CW00855338

BEGINNER'S
GUIDE TO STAMP COLLECTING

Frontispiece—*Sir Rowland Hill (1795–1879)*

BEGINNER'S GUIDE
TO
STAMP COLLECTING

by
COLIN NARBETH

LUTTERWORTH PRESS · LONDON

First published 1966
Second impression 1968
Revised edition 1969
Second impression 1971

ISBN 0 7188 0034 6

COPYRIGHT © 1966 COLIN NARBETH

Printed in Great Britain by
Cox & Wyman Ltd., London,
Reading and Fakenham

CONTENTS

LIST OF ILLUSTRATIONS

LIST OF ILLUSTRATIONS

ACKNOWLEDGEMENTS

The author would like to make particular acknowledgement to: Mr Kenneth F. Chapman, editor of *Stamp Collecting*; Mr K. Tranmer; Mr Arthur Blair, editor of *Stamp Magazine*; Stanley Gibbons Ltd.; The British Philatelic Association; photographer Mr Alexander Bareham; Mr D. Davidson Putwain; Mr C. L. Tunstill; Mr G. H. Penfold, M.A.; Mr B. Williams; Mr Frank Staff, who has supplied several photographs from his collection, and the many other collectors and professional philatelists who have helped him to compile this book.

The Frontispiece is reproduced with permission of H.M. Postmaster General.

INTRODUCTION

S TAMP collecting has a larger following than any other hobby in the world. Since 1840, when Great Britain issued the first adhesive postage stamps, collectors have swelled in numbers to a stage where they can literally influence governmental decisions to issue new stamps. Some small territories rely on the sale of their postage stamps to collectors for a considerable portion of their national income. In 1965 it was estimated that there were in Britain alone as many as 250,000 active collectors and that as many as four million of the population "dabbled" in stamps.

It is doubtful whether anyone can analyse the reasons that prompt a person to become a collector of anything; but a number of reasons can be advanced to show why stamp collecting enjoys such popularity.

Perhaps the most significant is that it is possible to collect stamps at no cost at all, or to spend many thousands of pounds on a single stamp. The most valuable stamp in the world is considered to be the unique 1 cent British Guiana, insured for £200,000—but some experts contend that it would not be likely to fetch more than £20,000 if the stamp ever came up for auction. Even so, £20,000 is a great deal of money for a piece of paper that size.

The field of rarities is not confined to experts and wealthy men. In 1965 a Scottish schoolboy bought a stamp for 6d. and sold it by auction for £380! He had noticed that the stamp, one of the issue commemorating the opening of the new Forth Road Bridge, was a freak with part of the background missing. Numerous flaws have been found on the Churchill stamps and subsequent issues, including some quite major flaws such as the Post Office Tower stamp with the tower completely missing.

1. *The most valuable stamp in the world. The one cent*
British Guiana

From this we can see that anyone can take up the hobby and form an interesting collection, regardless of any limitation in spending power. The young collector has a distinct advantage in the stamp world. His early years as a collector will enable him to overcome the pitfalls and mistakes all too often leapt into by more adult collectors who suddenly decide to take up the hobby as a relaxation.

Perhaps the most comforting thing about philately is that the collector can make his hobby as simple or as complicated as he likes. There is no need to fear that the hobby is too big or too difficult to understand. It can be as simple as collecting different pictures of flowers on stamps or as complicated as studying the stamps of one issue in such detail that their exact position on the original plate can be determined. (The "plate" is the name given to the designed metal from which the sheets of stamps are actually printed.)

The mere accumulation of a large number of stamps means very little in the philatelic world. It is possible to buy packets of 3,000 stamps for as little as 48s. 6d. and at least one dealer has offered for sale 95,000 different stamps of the world for £3,600—yet there are a number of individual stamps which would all fetch more than that. It is far better to have a small collection of clean, neatly postmarked and undamaged stamps properly mounted, than to have an enormous mass of stamps in damaged and dirty condition.

In 1866 there were fewer than three thousand different stamps to collect, but to-day the large number issued, constantly increased by new issues, makes it impossible to attempt a complete collection of the world with any reasonable hope of success. This has meant that collectors specialize, taking the stamps of only one country, a group of countries, a subject or even a set of stamps.

To get full enjoyment and benefit from a collection of stamps the beginner must have an inquisitive mind. With this as the basis of a collecting instinct, philately can provide all the interest that the mind can seek. This is perhaps why some of the world's most eminent men take to forming collections as a change from their professional activities, and as a means of exercising their minds.

An album of stamps can be a book of knowledge, a book of original research and a miniature stocks and shares market all rolled into one. There can be few subjects which are not illustrated by stamps and, without realizing it, the collector soon finds he is building up a know-ledge of geography, history and economics—in a far more interesting manner than from any school textbook!

The fact that there are a large number of stamp collectors all over the world means that apart from the fun of collecting, there is also a hard cash value in a stamp collection. Stamps are not subject to the inflation or deflation of a particular country, but will have a fairly con-stant value throughout the world. Like stocks and shares, stamps go up and down in value, though it is noticeable that the "downs" are seldom drastic and usually recover. The "ups" are so frequent that the *Financial Times* once devoted a page to the investment possibilities, showing that in a great number of cases the stamp investor was showing a far bigger return than the ordinary share buyer. So the beginner need not fear that he is wasting money buying stamps if he is wise in his purchases.

Investors who dabble in stamps often adversely affect the genuine collectors by trying to force prices up, and then flooding the market with an issue thought to be scarce.

Another reason for a drop in value of some stamps is the unfortunate habit of some governments of selling off their unsold stocks as "remainders" to dealers at below face value. Collectors who have paid a true market value for the stamp while it was in official use suddenly find it can be bought for less. However, despite these pitfalls, the world of stamps is a glorious share-market for those who want to invest as well as collect for fun.

Sudden appreciation in value of some stamps is due to the most unlikely reasons. For instance, the visit of the Queen of Tonga to England saw a sudden rise in the number of collectors of Tonga stamps. The volcanic eruption at Tristan Da Cunha turned the island into a popular specialist field.

In order to be able to form a collection of stamps intelligently there are certain things that the beginner must learn. He must come to understand the philatelist's vocabulary, and, to assist him at this stage, the diagrams opposite illustrate a few of the basic philatelic terms.

It is also important for the collector to understand something about the actual making and printing of a stamp. Indeed, for the collector interested in errors on stamps a study of the manufacture of stamps is essential as it enables him to differentiate between varieties which have little philatelic importance and those which are important.

PRINTING PROCESSES

There are four main printing processes used for the production of postage stamps. Typography, lithography, engraving and photogravure.

Typography

Typography is also known as letterpress or surface printing. It is a relief process. That is to say the design which is to be printed is higher on the printing plate than the non-printing surface. This of course, is the process by which the bulk of the world's books, papers and magazines are printed. Sometimes stamps printed by this method can be easily identified because the image is occasionally visibly depressed into the paper showing as raised portions on the back.

Triangular stamp   Diamond-shaped stamp

Vignette

Frame

Perforation   Face value

First day cover
postmark date is first day of issue

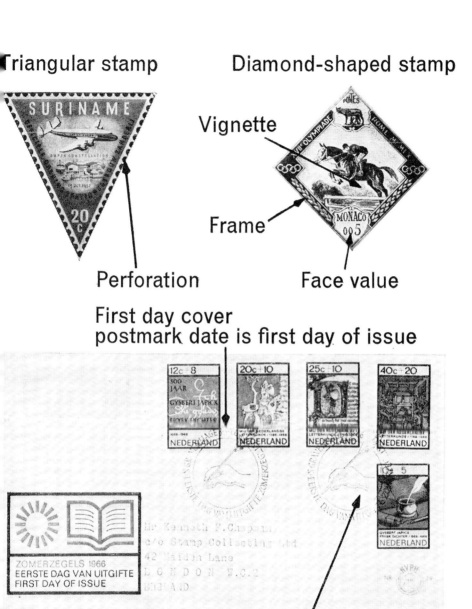

Stamp is "tied" to cover by postmark

2. Stamp terms

Some oddities of this process include the first issues of Uganda which were literally typewritten by the Rev. E. Millar at Mengo in 1895. Other unusual examples of typography include the handstamps used for printing Afghanistan early issues, and typeset stamps (as distinct from pictorial designs) such as the early Hawaii (the well-known "Missionary" stamps of 1851–52) and local postmasters' issues of the Confederate States. There are also stamps where the actual printing plate has been hand-engraved so that each design (or cliché) on the plate is hand-made as against machine-reproduced from a master die. These invariably differ from each other in some respects and are easily recognized under a magnifying glass.

But the bulk of stamps produced typographically come from plates which have been reproduced from a mould from a master die. The accuracy of detail in each design to the original is therefore far greater. The most common methods of reproduction from the original die are by stereotyping or electrotyping.

These methods produce their own types of differences which can sometimes be detected by philatelists. When the mould is made it sometimes happens that the die does not strike properly and the register is not accurate. This gives the effect of "doubling" part of the design and is known as a "double strike" variety.

During the process of electroplating the metal shell has to be removed from the wax mould, and occasionally its removal causes damage, however minute, which is faithfully reproduced when the plate is used to print stamps. Experts find such faults a great help in "plating"—reconstructing a sheet of stamps with each stamp in its correct position.

A variety often found on stereotyped stamps is the difference in sizes. This is caused during the cooling process of casting the stereos.

Lithography

Stamps printed by lithography (planographic process) means that the printing surface is on the same level as the non-printing surface. The printing area accepts the inks while the non-printing area rejects them because of special treatment based on the antipathy of grease to water. Where, as in the early days, the process involves the use of thin transfer paper, a number of varieties can occur due to creased transfers, and wrongly-placed transfers. Lithographically-produced stamps can sometimes be detected due to the homogeneous inked image resting

3. (a) *Typographic*

(b) *Typographic*

(c) *Recess (engraved). An example where two methods of printing were used in the same set. (France 1945–46)*

(d) *Lithographic*

(e) *Lithographic*

B

on the surface, with soft outlines. Modern offset printing does not need to use hand transfers and although the early litho issues are comparably easier to "plate", present day photo-lithography is very accurate and causes fewer varieties.

Engraved

Line engraved (intaglio) is the process where the engraved plate is recessed, that is to say the design which is to be produced is below the printing surface of the plate. This was the process used for the very first adhesive stamp, the 1840 Penny Black. Tremendous skill is required by the engraver who, using special tools, engraves the design into the die, cutting away slivers of steel. Certain plates have been entirely hand-engraved which enables philatelists to plate them easily since no engraver can produce two items exactly the same, as can be seen by magnification. But the majority were mechanically produced by a process invented by Jacob Perkins of Massachusetts and George Murray of Philadelphia who patented the "siderography" process in 1813. Their process enables steel engravings to be transferred to steel plates as many times as is needed.

This process causes certain varieties peculiar to the engraving system. While the transfer roll is placing the design on to the plate perfect adjustment is necessary or the design will "double" or "shift".

Difficult to tell from the "double" is the "fresh entry". This happens when one of the designs on the plate is out of alignment and is destroyed to be replaced by a new one. If the orignal design is not completely erased some of the lines are likely to show as well as the fresh entry.

It is also in the engraved issues that plating collectors get their best chance through the "re-entries". When the plate becomes worn or some of the designs damaged, the transfer roller is adjusted to coincide with the plate and the design is "sharpened up". Often such repairs are visible under a magnifying glass and are called "re-entries".

Sometimes, and particularly among the early issues, worn engraved plates etc. were repaired by hand. This is called "recutting" and is really hand tooling to correct a fault as against a re-entry which is made by machinery. Rotary-press plates can only be "retouched", which implies that lines of the design have been strengthed by the use of acid,

18

since once the plate has been curved and hardened it would not be possible to recut or re-enter.

Cracks cause "hair-line" varieties on stamps. These occur because of the severe strains put on plates during processing. Gouging and scratches, caused by accidents to the plate, also leave their marks and are of importance in plating stamps.

Line engraved stamps, under magnification, can often be easily identified because the design inked image stands above the paper surface and, sometimes, the back of the stamp clearly shows a depression where the design work is.

Photogravure

This is also an intaglio process, but here the work is done photographically. The design is photographed and reduced to the size wanted and the negative is used to produce the number of positives wanted to make up a plate. This process is so well produced that very few varieties occur. Some that do include "positive retouches" which are caused when there is a blot on the negative which is retouched out. Such retouches would then occur on

1   *Photogravure: United Nations Children's Fund stamp*

all sheets printed from plates made by that positive. When the cylinder is damaged it can be retouched and this causes varieties on stamps printed from that particular cylinder. This process is known by various names, photogravure, photo, heliogravure, and rotogravure. Under a magnifying glass, photogravure-printed stamps can be seen to consist of minute dots of colour, separated by white spaces caused by the screen through which the image is transferred to the printing cylinder or plate.

Another process for printing stamps is embossing, which has been used for much of the world's postal stationery. An interesting variety occurs in this process known as an "albino". It happens when two sheets of paper go into the press at the same time. One sheet gets the embossed image complete with coloured inks but the other sheet is embossed without colour.

Some varieties occur in most of the processes under certain circumstances. These are inverted centres, printed on both sides, and the "kiss"—where during removal of the sheet from a plate it touches the plate again.

It will be seen how important it is to study the printing methods if the collector is interested in acquiring these types of varieties. Many collectors have considerable difficulty in identifying the various processes. One way to do it is to build up a "library collection" by getting stamps of a known process (the main catalogues list the processes for each issue) and then compare them with others. Then the collector will be better placed to identify stamps which have been produced by two different methods—as sometimes happens.

In the course of time, many famous collections have been formed. Perhaps the most famous collection of all time was that formed by an Austrian who lived in Paris, M. Philipp la Renotière von Ferrari. When the 1914–18 war broke out he sought refuge in Switzerland and died there before the end of the war. The French Government seized his property and his stamp collection, which had taken him 40 years to compile, was auctioned for 26 million francs. At that auction Arthur Hind of Utica, New York, bought the 1 cent British Guiana (which once changed hands for six shillings) for $37,000 for his collection, and later also acquired the fairly famous Duveen collection of Mauritius and the Griebert collection of Spain. On his death his collection, less the rarest stamp in the world, was sold for a million dollars in 1933–34. And it must be remembered that this sale took place during the world's worst financial depression.

The Tapling collection was bequeathed to the British Museum and is probably the most important collection in any museum, though many European capitals have exceptionally fine collections on display, as well as United States institutions.

King Farouk of Egypt formed an extensive collection which included many rarities. When he was deposed the Egyptian Government auctioned the collection which was avidly bought up by dealers from all over the world. A late president of the United States, Franklin D. Roosevelt, also formed a collection which attracted much attention when it was sold on his death. Many of the covers from this collection are stamped "From the Roosevelt collection".

Undoubtedly the most valuable collection in private hands in Great Britain is that of Queen Elizabeth II. The collection is housed in more than 350 albums and worth well over a £1 million. The Queen employs Sir John Wilson as Keeper of her collection. From time to time sections of the Royal collection are put on public exhibition.

The world's great rarities in stamps are known and tabulated as well as the fingerprint department of Scotland Yard! The top dealers in the world know which collections have them and, indeed, the entire history of such rarities. As a result of this, stolen rarities have sometimes been recovered. There is one instance where a dealer telephoned a big collector because he had seen a rarity on the market known to have been in his collection—the collector only then realized that it had been stolen!

5. *The Goya nude which "shocked" a nation*

Some stamps, and not necessarily rare ones, have interesting stories behind their issue and linked with their postal careers. Such a stamp is the Spanish issue bearing the famous Goya nude painting commonly assumed to be of the Duchess of Alba. American congressmen were shocked when mail bearing these stamps first came to the United States and made serious efforts to have such mail banned from entry into the country.

As well as the history of the postage stamp, many philatelists study the history of the posts and this takes us back to the very beginning of history itself. Indeed, the "Father of History", Herodotus, describing the Persian postal system, wrote: "Neither snow nor rain nor heat nor gloom of night stays these couriers from the swift completion of their appointed rounds"—and this quotation has been carved over the entrances to some post offices.

The romance of the posts takes the collector to every part of the world, from the Wells Fargo Pony Express to the balloon mail in besieged Paris in the Franco-Prussian war of 1870–71.

In the world of philately, whatever the future portends, Stanley Gibbons will forever be remembered as the man who did more for it than anybody else. Today the firm of Stanley Gibbons Ltd., which publish the main philatelic catalogues for this country, employ a large number of people and incorporate Harmer, Rooke and Co. Ltd*., one of the world's best known philatelic auctioneers. In 1965 the firm celebrated its centenary of catalogue issues—and to mark the occasion one Arab country actually issued a set of stamps showing Stanley Gibbons catalogues to commemorate the centenary. But the firm's beginnings were very humble—in the corner of a Plymouth chemist's shop owned by Stanley Gibbons' father. As a boy, Edward Stanley Gibbons was allowed to trade in stamps in part of the shop.

One day two sailors walked into the shop with a kit-bag full of Cape of Good Hope Triangulars. They wanted five pounds for them, and Gibbons gladly paid. The sailors, who said they had won the stamps in a shilling raffle, were more than pleased—and so was Gibbons. They started him on the road to being the most important stamp dealer in the world. Although, it is said, he made around five hundred pounds profit on the stamps, some of them today fetch more than one thousand pounds each.

* Now changed in name to Stanley Gibbons' Auctions Ltd.

A DESCRIPTIVE

PRICE LIST & CATALOGUE

OF

BRITISH, COLONIAL & FOREIGN

POSTAGE STAMPS,

FOR SALE BY

E. STANLEY GIBBONS,

FOREIGN POSTAGE STAMP DEALER,

15, TREVILLE STREET,

PLYMOUTH.

This List will be sent to any address in the Kingdom, post free, for 2d. ;
or abroad, post free, for 5d.

Plymouth:
COVE BROTHERS, PRINTERS, &c., 9, TREVILLE STREET.

6. Stanley Gibbons' first catalogue—November 1865

In 1865 Stanley Gibbons produced his first catalogue, which was a penny price-list, *Descriptive Price List and Catalogue of British, Colonial and Foreign Postage Stamps for sale by E. Stanley Gibbons*. Today, this catalogue is worth a great deal to collectors for its own rarity. Only two copies are known. The Penny Black, the first adhesive postage stamp, was priced in this catalogue at 1d. used and 6d. for a dozen. One hundred years later the most common copy of the Penny Black is catalogued by Stanley Gibbons Ltd. at 75s. Damaged and poor copies with heavy obliterations can often be bought for less, but even bad copies fetch 10s. each, and superb copies fetch well above Stanley Gibbons' catalogue price.

Today there are hundreds of large dealers all over the world offering an excellent service to collectors; there are clubs in many towns throughout Great Britain and there are societies for nearly every possible type of specialization where men and women, with a common collector's interest, can get together to enjoy the most popular hobby in the world.

In recent months the Government of Great Britain has taken notice of the stamp world. The monotonous little stamps that graced our letters have been transformed into colourful, modernistic pictorials commemorating a wide variety of subjects from the new Post Office Tower to the Salvation Army. Criticism of the designs, and there has been much, is academic. The great majority of collectors welcome these colourful stamps and it opens out a new field for collectors who live in Great Britain. In 1965 alone, hundreds of varieties of these commemorative stamps were discovered, some valued at a few pence and some at hundreds of pounds. The new collector might well examine the post that comes to his home for he might find a missing value, a missing part of design and so on.

CHAPTER 1

ANATOMY OF A STAMP

T HE collector having identified the country of origin of a stamp (see Appendix 1), now faces what can be the most difficult task of all—deciding exactly which issue the stamp came from.

There are many stamps, particularly commemoratives, where there was only one issue of a certain design. In such cases the philatelist has no trouble. His catalogue will tell him which set the stamp belongs to, its date of issue and the perforation and watermark. The problem arises when, under the type of design in the catalogue, the collector finds several stamps that appear to be exactly the same but for differences in perforation, paper, colour or watermark. Every type of stamp in the catalogue will be numbered and it is important to the collector that he can find out precisely which catalogue number represents his stamp.

It is necessary because one stamp may be, and often is, very much rarer than another. The difference between an issue of stamps of perforation 12 or $12\frac{1}{2}$—hardly noticeable to the eye—can mean a difference of many pounds in cash value because, perhaps, only a few stamps were issued with one perforation while large numbers were issued with the other.

Some stamps are very difficult indeed to "place" and experts have trouble with them as well as beginners! When philatelists recognize a collector as an expert it is because that person has studied his chosen field in great depth. He has handled hundreds of rare stamps and noted minute differences—even to the point of identifying the position of a stamp on the plate. That means he can sometimes tell exactly what position in a sheet of stamps an individual stamp occupied, which plate (and there may be many) printed the sheet and, even, by studying retouches, which printing from that plate the stamp came from. Experience and continual handling of stamps is the only real way to find out about certain unusual issues, and no advice to a beginner is a substitute for this. If, for instance, a stamp is catalogued with five different shades of green, the beginner with a single stamp will find it hard to judge its true colour. If he has all five to look at he is better able to determine which one is light blue-green and which one is blue-green. The man who has handled hundreds of each will recognize each shade instantly, without having to think. This is one reason why the beginner should seize every opportunity of examining collections and exhibitions. The more stamps he sees the more he learns, even if only subsconsciously.

When the full difficulty of matching certain issues with a catalogue number is appreciated, the collector can set about learning to distinguish the minute differences of the stamps he collects. The majority of stamps can be catalogued with a little patience and thought. As with any other hobby a little help from more experienced collectors is invaluable. First find out which stamp you think it is, then ask an experienced collector. If you are wrong, find out where the "detection" went astray so that the difficulty with that particular issue does not arise again. The collector who simply asks what stamp he has and goes away without knowing why it is a certain issue has learned nothing.

PERFORATIONS

Stamps which have straight edges are called "imperforate" as against perforated stamps—though where a stamp is actually described as "straight edges" it denotes that perforated edges have been cut (as often happens in stamp booklets). Also, early issues of some countries were both perforated and imperforate. Where the imperforate is worth very much more, collectors try and get copies with "wide margins" as it is not unknown for someone to cut the edges off a perforated issue to make it appear a rare imperforate issue.

Perforations are very important in classifying a stamp. If we take the 1890 issues of Austria as an example, there are about 40 different perforations or combinations of perforation in this one set. A stamp identical except for the difference in perforation can be worth 4d. in one case and a pound in another, because of its relative rarity.

Before you go into the sizes of a perforation it is necessary to understand something about edging of stamps in general. First then, establish which sort of edging the stamp has. It may be imperforate, perforated or rouletted—which, like perforation, cuts the paper, but unlike perforation does not take away any paper.

The 1840 Penny Black of Great Britain was the first adhesive postage

26

stamp and had no perforation at all. These stamps were printed in sheets and the post office clerks were obliged to cut each stamp from the sheet with scissors. It was a time-consuming job, and it was not long before various methods were introduced so that the stamps could be easily torn from the sheet.

The first attempts at solving the problem of clerks having to cut out stamps were confined to rouletting. The essential difference between a roulette and a perforation is that the rouletting does not remove any part of the paper and the perforation does. Even so, some issues are hard to detect and comparatively recently experts decided that an issue of Finland was not a perforation but a roulette!

The main forms of rouletting are:

Arc rouletting. A method in which cuts were made in curved lines. A very fine form of arc rouletting is known as "serrating".

Diamond or lozenge rouletting. Cuts are made in the shape of little crosses which produce diamond or lozenge shapes at the stamp edges.

Pin rouletting. Tiny holes are pricked into the paper, without, however, any paper being removed.

Line rouletting. This is made with straight-line cuts with gaps between each cut.

Colour rouletting. When notched, curved metal rules were set between the clichés forming the plate. These rules were then inked in various colours and, as the sheets were printed, slightly cut into the margins of the stamps.

Saw-tooth rouletting (also known as *zig-zag rouletting*). In this the cuts look like the edge of a saw blade.

Serpentine rouletting. Wavy lines are cut between the stamps.

With the introduction of perforating machines the rouletting of stamps largely ceased—though some countries continued rouletting for many years. There are three main types of perforation.

Line perforation. In this method each row of stamps is perforated separately and, on a sheet of a hundred stamps, eleven strokes are necessary to perforate them horizontally and another eleven to perforate vertically. It means that stamps with line perforations are usually found with irregular corners and on blocks the uneven intersections, which cause the irregular corners, are easily seen.

Harrow perforation. Here the punches are so arranged that they perforate the whole sheet at once. Naturally they have even holes and the corners are all alike, but they present a great difficulty to the authorities. If the paper is not placed exactly in position, every stamp on the sheet is out of centre. Harrow perforation restricts the authorities to a certain size of stamp, whereas other methods can be used on any size. Certain countries, such as Hungary and Austria, have numerous harrow perforations. The edge corners of a single stamp look regular (which is not so with the line-perforated stamp) but, because of the process of perforating, the majority of the stamps are slightly off-centre. It is sometimes very difficult to tell the difference between a single stamp harrow-perforated against a single stamp comb-perforated when the design is well-centred because it resembles the comb perforation.

Comb perforation. This is the method by which most modern stamps are perforated. The punches are arranged like the teeth of a comb in one horizontal row, with small rows at right-angles the length of a single stamp, and each short row is the width of a single stamp from its neighbour.

Starting at the top of a sheet, the first drop of the punch perforates the top and the two sides of the stamps in the first horizontal row—then the sheet is moved upwards and the process is repeated so that the top of the second row is also the bottom of the first row. In this manner the sheet is fully perforated.

So comb perforated stamps are usually well-centred, with regular corners. In multiples showing the sheet edge they are easily distinguished from harrow perforation multiples because the bottom of the sheet is always perforated by the comb system, but never with the harrow system.

Varieties. The different kinds of machines used for perforating can cause certain varieties. The Guillotine line perforator requires 22 strokes to perforate a sheet. If the machinist is not watching properly, eleven strokes may be applied horizontally and the sheet passed on without the eleven vertical strokes, causing part-perforated stamps. Also, if a stroke is missed, the division between pairs of stamps can become imperforate.

Rotary. The rotary line perforator is made up of sets of wheels mounted on shafts. Because of the technical difficulties two machines are often used together, one for the horizontal perforation and one for the vertical. But bad adjustment can lead to oversize or undersize perforations.

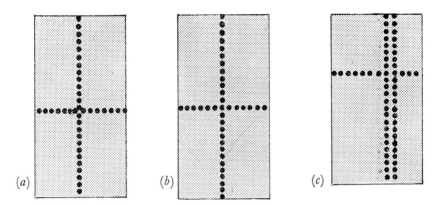

7. (a) *Line perforation. (Irregular intersection)*
(b) *Comb perforation. (Perfect intersection)*
(c) *Double perforation error*

Interrupted perforation. This is met with on certain stamps, particularly issues of Danzig and the Netherlands which were prepared for vending machines. The perforations were done by comb perforating machines and certain pins were taken away to produce the interruptions in the line of perforation.

Rough perforations. These occur when the pins of the machine become worn.

Blind perforations. This is a term used to differentiate between an imperforate stamp and one where the machine has not been properly adjusted so that the pins do not meet the holes. They then "dent" the paper only.

Double perforation. Sometimes the sheet is not moved properly and it is possible for the perforator to make two strokes almost on the same line.

Fantails. Although not applicable to the harrow machine, other methods sometimes omit to perforate the marginal edge of the outer row. This gives an imperforate margin known as a "fantail".

Freaks. These are not regarded in the same light as varieties because they seldom re-occur with any matching regularity. Occasionally a sheet is put through the machine with an edge folded or fed into the

8. *An example of a freak perforation caused by a fold in the paper*

machine at an angle causing such perforation. They are rarely found because the officials normally remove and destroy such sheets before issuing stamps to the post offices.

Mixed perforations. Where the workmanship goes slightly wrong some sheets are re-perforated using a different gauge. Hard to distinguish from a double perforation, they can be identified where the gauge of the perforation can be seen.

Compound perforations. These occur when different gauges are used for the vertical and horizontal sides. There are many examples of compound perforations especially among early British colonial stamps and some mid-European countries, like Austria, where an enormous number of variations are known.

Gauges. Once the type of perforation is established, the collector must find out the gauge, and to do this he needs a perforation gauge. There are several types. The gauge number is determined by the number of holes that fill a two – centimetre space. The types of equipment and method of use are described in Chapter 5.

PAPER

Besides having differences in perforation many stamps are made with different types of paper and some can only be distinguished by the paper.

The only effective way to tell the difference is by handling the various sorts of paper and getting accustomed to them. The main types are:

Wove. An even-grained paper produced by feeding the pulped fibre of which paper is made on to a fine wire screen. Some early stamps were printed on hand-wove paper.

Laid paper. Fairly easy to distinguish, though it is not so easy to differentiate between hand-made and machine-made varieties. Here the paper has laid lines. If he holds it up to the light the collector can see dark and light lines in the paper.

Batonné. Seldom met with in the stamp world, this type of paper is distinguished by a line at wide intervals. It is found in both wove and laid papers. On wove it has a light line, and on laid paper a darker, stronger line. Certain Afghanistan and Indian State stamps have the batonné paper.

Pelure. This is a very thin paper and is nearly transparent, though often brittle. The word is French and means "copying paper", which is perhaps the best way of describing it.

Quadrillé. Very seldom met with on stamps, but in 1892 it was used for the 15 centimes stamp of France. It is easily recognized as it is a pattern of squares. The majority of loose-leaf album sheets have a quadrille pattern to help collectors measure their lay-out.

Card. Sometimes card is used for stamps and is naturally easy to recognize when felt.

Granite paper. Used by various countries, particularly in Europe, this is paper which is more grey than white, a quality produced by silk fibres being compressed and evenly spread.

Chalk paper. When held at a certain angle to the light, chalk-papered stamps shine. The surface has a coating of chalk, intended to prevent the re-use of the stamp.

Some papers, such as silk thread paper where one or more strands of coloured silk run through the stamp, are very easily identified (though sometimes they are difficult to see). This also applies to double paper, where two layers of paper have been joined; coloured papers, enamelled papers, varnished papers and ribbed papers.

GUM

The gum on the back of a stamp can also help to determine which issue the stamp belongs to. It happens that some stamps were issued, and still are, without any gum at all. China is a modern example of this, but some early issues of Curaçao were left without gum because of the effect the tropical climate was expected to have upon them. Sometimes in emergencies, like the Japanese earthquake in 1923, there are ungummed issues.

At first, gum was applied by hand. This can be distinguished from machine gumming by traces of brush strokes. Detecting the difference can help to place certain early issues of Canada. Philatelists note differences in gum by describing them as smooth, crackly, ribbed or streaked.

WATERMARKS

Often the most significant factor in identification, watermarks are made during the manufacture of paper. A watermark can generally

9. *Typical watermarks*

be seen by holding the stamp up to the light and looking at the back of the stamp. There are watermark detectors (see page 68) and some watermarks are quite difficult to detect.

At first the single watermark was most commonly used, but this presented great difficulty to the printers. Everything had to be exact or the single watermarks would not fall in the centre of each stamp. Another difficulty was that stamps vary in size and shape and it meant producing a special watermark "dandy roll" with watermarks to fit each size during the making of the paper. The multiple watermark was introduced to overcome this problem. Some countries use a sheet watermark, where a single design or word is used for the entire sheet. Many Austrian stamps have the word "Briefmarken" in large letters on the sheet. To collectors this means that stamps from that sheet can be collected without watermarks, with bits of watermarked letters, or most desirable of all, with a complete letter of the watermark, and are valued accordingly.

There are many varieties of watermarks. They can be inverted, reversed and sometimes both inverted and reversed.

When the collector has satisfied himself that the stamp under consideration belongs to a certain issue, and he knows its perforation, paper and watermark, he is faced with the question, "Is it a good copy?"

CHAPTER 2

EXAMINING A STAMP

O FTEN the collector will be able to make a choice from a number of copies of the same stamp. Selecting the most desirable copy is the real art of the stamp collector, and a glance at a selected collection will reveal the knowledge, ability and artistic taste of the compiler. Anyone, with enough money, can collect rare and expensive stamps, but a discerning collector can create a desirable collection.

It must be remembered that the choice of a stamp is a personal matter and there are collectors who do not mind if a stamp is damaged —if they like it they put it in their collection. The majority, however, reject a stamp in bad condition unless it is extremely rare, and some refuse a stamp if there is any defect at all.

The standard for selecting a "choice" item is, really, the same as for any other collectable item. As long as there are connoisseurs there is only one acceptable standard—perfection. This means that the item, whatever it may be, should be as near to its original state of issue as possible. So a stamp with an imperfect design caused by bad printing can, nevertheless, be collected as a "perfect" specimen of that printing error.

Of course, there are exceptions to every rule. Numismatists prefer to have a patina on ancient coins even though they could clean it off to restore the item to its original state. But the patina protects the coin, so it is desirable. And the philatelist does not rub a postmark off a stamp to restore it to its original state—because the postmark tells a story, sometimes more interesting than the stamp itself and because the gum on the back of the stamp could not be put back except by forgery.

The standard of a stamp is reflected in its actual cash value to collectors. A stamp which in perfect condition would fetch £20 at auction can usually be expected to fetch only a few shillings if it is damaged. Naturally there are exceptions, such as a stamp of great rarity of which it would be impossible to get a "perfect" copy. In that case the least damaged stamp of that issue must set the standard for that item.

Bearing in mind that every rule can be made flexible, no collector can go wrong in demanding the best he can possibly get. Experts can enhance a collection with a second-best specimen, included to demonstrate an unusual variety or flaw, but beginners are more likely to spoil a collection with such additions.

When, shortly after 1840, people first started saving stamps, they gave little thought to the back of the stamp. For one thing, no one dreamed of the enormous value that stamps would one day attain, and the majority of the educated community regarded such collectors as cranks. The stamp hinge had not been invented and consequently many people stuck stamps down with paste. Those stamps are virtually valueless today because they cannot be restored to their original state.

As the hobby progressed, differences in perforation, watermarks and paper were noted by the keener collectors and soon attention was given to the condition of the back of a stamp as well as to its front. When the stamp hinge was invented it was felt that this was the finest, most enjoyable way of mounting stamps. Collectors could lay their stamps out attractively on pages and embellish them as they would. The fact that the hinge would leave a mark on the back of a mint stamp was not considered serious enough to outweigh the advantages of displaying stamps mounted on hinges.

This was all very understandable and it would be true to state that the majority of collectors adhere to this view today. But perfectionists would not accept it. As early as the 1930's some Continental collectors contended that the English were damaging the backs of their stamps with hinge marks and, instead of using hinges, they used the "stock album" system in which stamps are placed in rows of transparent pockets. This, of course, greatly reduced flexibility of lay-out, and the English continued with their hinges unabashed.

Only a few years ago, however, the Continentals invented the "strips" which allow mint stamps to be mounted on album pages without being harmed in any way. These strips consist of a length of black paper, gummed on one side for adhering to the page of the album. The front of the black paper has an acetate type window open at the top so that the stamp can be inserted and held securely. The effect was immediate. The word "unmounted" crept into the dealers' price-lists on an unprecedented scale. There was no reason now why the perfectionist should not have his stamp in perfect mint condition and still enjoy the same freedom in displaying his collection as the man who used hinges.

The philatelic press was bombarded by letters from elderly philatelists, who, for the greater part of their lives, had steadfastly fastened stamps down with hinges. This new vogue, they contended, was fastidious. It was carrying things too far. Where was it all going to stop? In any case it would be impossible to get many of the earlier stamps in unmounted condition, so how could it affect their value?

The controversy still goes on. The majority of collectors use hinges but now pay very much more attention to ensuring that there is only a light hinge mark on the back of their stamps. Heavily hinged stamps are frowned on. The perfectionist got his way in one respect. The standard that applies to all collectable items applied to the back of the stamp. Unmounted they fetch better prices and dealers, on average, charge 15 per cent more for an unmounted stamp. In short, an unmounted stamp is worth more because it is that much better!

This gives an idea of the requirements of a choice stamp, the difference between a first-class stamp and a second-best. So, when you are examining a stamp it is a good idea to start by looking at the front and back to see that there is no damage at all. If there is a light hinge mark on a mint stamp, it is acceptable, but not perfect. If there is a light hinge mark on a used stamp, it is completely acceptable, because in fact the mark can be taken off. Were such a mark taken off a mint stamp, the gum would have to be damaged.

Hold the stamp up to the light so that any defect in the paper such as a pin-hole or "thinning" can be spotted. Next, see that the stamp is well-centred. A perfect copy should have the design of the stamp placed equi-distant from the edges. Many stamps have wider margins between the design and perforation on one side than on the other. They are not well-centred and therefore are not so good. However, there are certain exceptions to this rule. There are stamps that are worth very much more off-centre than well-centred, simply because in those particular issues the vast majority were well-centred. Even so, such stamps are few and far between and the beginner cannot go far wrong in wanting his stamps well-centred.

The case of Iceland is an exception worth mentioning. Finding a well-centred Icelandic stamp of the early issues is virtually impossible.

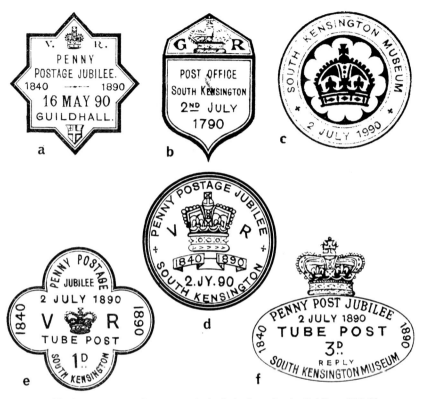

10. *Early commemorative postmarks include those for the Jubilee of Uniform Penny Postage*

(a) *The Guildhall cancellation*

(b) *An old-time Post Office of 1790 was part of the South Kensington exhibition and a specially dated postmark was issued for this Post Office*

(c) *A novelty postmark of the Post Office of the future*

(d) *The South Kensington Museum cancellation*

(e) and (f) *Tube post cancellations*

When such stamps do appear they are usually found to be reperforated stamps.

Postmarks

On used stamps the postmark has a variety of effects to the collector. It can be that the postmark is more important than the stamp. For example, on a common stamp the postmark of a letter posted on board ship, military post offices abroad, or a commemorative postmark, could make it more interesting. In such cases the collector is more interested in seeing a perfect postmark than worried about the way the postmark affects the stamp.

But where the main purpose of the postmark, so far as the collector is concerned, is to show that the stamp is cancelled, he is particular about the way the cancellation affects the stamp. If the main part of the design is obliterated by a heavy parcel-post cancellation, the stamp is no longer desirable. Where the stamp is lightly marked, without interfering with the visual attractiveness of the design, the stamp is worth more than the normally cancelled stamp.

Forgery

If the stamp under examination is of exceptional value, the examination to see whether it is desirable would have to be very much more thorough. Expert repairs on a damaged stamp can often be seen only under special lamps. Such repairs would only be carried out on valuable stamps. It is even possible to forge watermarks. This field of inspection is so complicated that a beginner is better advised to seek expert opinion on a valuable stamp. Colours can be faked, overprints added, postmarks taken off and any number of tricks employed against the collector.

Like "cops and robbers" it has been a battle of wits ever since stamps fetched enough money to make it worthwhile forging them. The collector uses the inventions of science to determine if a stamp is genuine but, besides science, he needs experience. Forgery as such is dealt with more thoroughly in Chapter 10, and at this stage the only "forgery" a beginner need concern himself with is that which appertains to ordinary stamps. The word is used to mean anything which is not in fact the original stamp issued for postal service. Some stamps, of course, are not in fact forgeries as they were not produced for the purpose of

deceiving. But as many of the official reprints are accepted by un-
suspecting collectors as the original issue, it seems fair to treat them as
such for the purpose of identification.

Unfortunately, in recent years, much has been done to provide the
collector with something that looks like what he wants but, in reality,
is not. Here are some:

Cancelled to order

The main forgery of this kind is the "cancelled to order" stamp.
Because the value of a used stamp is enhanced by a light postmark,
ways have been found to organize the light cancellation of stamps without their in fact passing through the post or even, for that matter, being
stuck on an envelope.

Whole sheets of stamps reach English dealers from places like Ghana,
Russia and Hungary in which cancellations have been placed neatly in
the centre join of each block of four stamps so that a quarter postmark
appears at a corner of each stamp only. In many cases the gum is still
intact on the backs of the unbroken sheets. There is no doubt that the
philatelic trade allows these cancelled to order stamps to go on the
market without much outcry. The main benefits, of course, belong to
the dealer, who can get these stamps without all the bother of having
to remove used stamps from their paper before he can sell them.

But, if a collector buys a stamp expecting it to be a used copy sent
through the post, when in reality it is cancelled to order, he has simply
been swindled. Some serious philatelists contend that if the sale of
cancelled-to-order stamps is advertised as "used postage stamps" the
vendor could be liable to prosecution for a sale by false pretences. Unfortunately they are usually advertised simply as "stamps".

Thus where a collector has a stamp with a fractional postmark
neatly clipping the corner, he is often going to have difficulty in
establishing whether it bears a genuine postmark or is cancelled to
order.

The problem of the cancelled-to-order stamp is getting more involved
and more difficult—sometimes impossible—to detect. Although many
countries have practised this type of deception upon the collector,
Great Britain has so far remained aloof. But in 1964 the G.P.O. showed
a tendency to pander to the collector by unfair means when they
offered a first-day cover service of the set of Shakespeare quater-

centenary stamps. In itself the first day cover service was a good thing. They cancelled stamps to order by ensuring that the postmark was light and did not mar the stamps, but the envelopes bearing these postmarks went through the post. This is a different sort of cancellation and is like an enthusiast going to the post office of his local town and asking them to lightly cancel his letters because they were for a collection. But the G.P.O. offered a first-day service for the Shakespeare issue on April 23, 1964. They received 80,000 orders and had to draft extra staff to cope with such a large amount. To satisfy the demand, they kept on using April 23 postmarks until as late as April 28. So a collector who received an April 23 postmark which was actually cancelled on April 28 was not getting a genuine first-day cover.

Remainders

Apart from the cancelled-to-order problem, collectors also have to distinguish postage stamps from remainders. It often happens that when a country has finished with a certain issue of stamps it is left with considerable stocks of the issue. These are sometimes sold to the philatelic trade as "remainders" and account for many stamps in mint condition being sold at less than face value. Some governments, aware of the collector, or to prevent their re-use, have cancelled the stamps in such a way that collectors can easily distinguish between them and normal used stamps. An example of this is the remainders of North Borneo and Labuan which were cancelled with postmarks consisting of black bars arranged so that each stamp received a part of the bars in one corner. This meant that collectors would know that the postmarks on such stamps were not in use during those stamps' postal service. Naturally, they are not worth so much. Ghana went to the other extreme and cancelled remainders with various different postmarks— the result being that they are indistinguishable from genuine used stamps. Stanley Gibbons has refused to catalogue them because of this and many collectors hope that the actions of such important firms as Stanley Gibbons will oblige offenders to cease the practice.

Great Britain has steadfastly avoided this problem by allowing all stocks to be used up in postal service and do service alongside more modern issues. In fact, all British stamps of King George V (from 1911 onwards) are still valid for postage. Sierra Leone has lately taken to overprinting her surplus stamps as commemoratives etc., to avoid being left with remainders. This has resulted in stamps of various different sets being used to form a new set, bearing appropriate overprints.

This is not the case with many countries, particularly in Central and South America. Quite early in the history of philately the governments of Honduras, Nicaragua, Salvador and Ecuador realized the profits to be made from selling stamps to collectors.

Several of these countries actually made a contract with a Mr. N. F. Seebeck who arranged to supply them with a new issue of stamps every year. When the issues were withdrawn and demonetized he was to have the stocks on hand and—of all things—the printing plates. Such stamps are known among philatelists as "Seebecks". He did very well out of the deal and when stocks ran short he simply printed very many more which can only be detected by small differences in shade! These "Seebecks" were found (around 1890–1900) in practically every mixed packet of stamps sold by dealers everywhere.

Reprints

It also happens that some countries, China for instance, find an issue of stamps sells very well to collectors and runs short. Although the issue is finished as far as postal service is concerned, to supply the demand they reprint the stamp. However, most of these can be detected from the original printings by slight differences in the printing of the design. These are usually listed in catalogues. Again there is a difference in value.

To collectors, reprints can be a little more complicated than they seem. Some are worth much more than the original issues! This occurs where reprints are made for a specific purpose other than simply to sell large quantities to collectors. Collectors seek certain reprints—such as the Berne reprints—as avidly as ordinary postage stamps. When Iceland issued the Gildi overprints it was customary to send specimen sets to the Universal Postal Union in Berne, Switzerland. When the Icelandic Government received a request for these stamps it was found that none was left. The Thiele Printing Company of Copenhagen was commissioned to reprint the stamps for the U.P.U. Some of these reprints can fetch well over a hundred pounds a set. Among the more famous reprints are those of the first issues of Nova Scotia, reprinted in 1890, and Heligoland where reprints are numerous and of little value. The latter were made privately by printers in Hamburg after Heligoland ceased to be British (in 1890) and German stamps were used in place of the former Heligoland stamps.

When the potential of the stamp market is taken into account it is not really surprising that all these reprints and cancelled to order stamps appear, but for the collector of genuine postage stamps they impose yet another trial of skill in detection.

Miniature Sheets

An increasing number of countries also issue miniature sheets of stamps. These are intended more as souvenirs—and pander to the collector. But at least they are openly produced and do not pretend to be issued for postal service, though they can be used on mail. It should be said that stamps in miniature sheets are exactly the same as those of normal sheets, in size. It is the sheet itself that is reduced in size. Sometimes there may be only one stamp in a miniature sheet, whereas the regular issue is produced with 100 stamps to the sheet. Countries such as Hungary go as far as to issue a miniature sheet, perforated and imperforate, of the same stamp, strictly controlling the number of issues to maintain their value in the stamp world. They are sold by the government offices at many times face value.

Until 1936 the miniature sheets were issued in very limited numbers. From then on more and more appeared, as country after country realized the income to be derived from them.

By and large, they are popular with collectors although until recently they were omitted from some catalogues on the grounds that they were not really intended for postal service at all. However, they do enhance a thematic collection where, after all, the design on the stamp is the most important item. And, of course, there is no reason why collectors should not collect remainders, cancelled to order stamps, reprints and miniature sheets. The only objection the serious philatelist has is where such an issue is offered in such a way that the collector believes he is getting the genuine postage stamp, and in fact is not.

A preliminary examination of a stamp is necessary to identify it; a second careful examination will make sure that the stamp is what it appears to be and that it is in good condition.

CHAPTER 3

THE POSTAGE STAMP

SINCE World War II the postage rates in England have risen from 2½d. to 4d.—to angry protests—yet to send a letter from London to Edinburgh for 4d. is very cheap when compared with the price of a box of matches, a cigarette or a cabbage! Moreover, it is very much less than it used to be! In 1839, just before the introduction of the postage stamp, it cost 1s. 1d. to send a one-ounce letter on that same journey from London to Edinburgh.

Several events led to the introduction of a postage stamp to show that the charges for letter delivery were paid. In the seventeenth century, de Villayer of Paris had invented wrappers which had stamps to show that postage was paid. In England, William Dockwra had used the now famous "Penny Post Paid" handstamps to the same end. Early in the 1800's Sardinia introduced letter-sheets with embossed stamps— not for postal charges but for tax to the government.

By 1835 serious consideration was being given to postal reforms in England. Committees were set up and report after report made.

Then, in January 1837, Rowland Hill, who is commemorated on many stamps of the world, produced his pamphlet on Post Office reform advocating a uniform penny postage charged at the beginning of a letter's journey. The wrapper, that had been used two centuries earlier in France, was put forward and, almost as an alternative, the adhesive postage stamp was suggested.

His pamphlet persuaded the government to set up another committee to examine his proposals. To the general public the suggestion for adhesive stamps and pre-paid wrappers were incidental, the main purpose of the reform being to establish a uniform penny rate. Until then, cost had been related to distance and charges were so high that the average person could not afford to send letters, and many were carried by private travellers to save expense. This is reflected in Rowland Hill's statement that despite a population increase of around 30 per cent between 1815 and 1825 there had been no increase in post office revenue. When his uniform penny postage was introduced in 1840 some 169 million letters were posted as against 76 million in 1839.

There was opposition to Rowland Hill's plans: the opposition that meets every new idea, but in 1839 Parliament passed the Uniform Penny Postage Act and on January 10, 1840, it was put into effect. Initially the postage rate had to be paid in cash and the letters handstamped as no adhesive stamp had then been produced.

The Treasury sponsored a competition in September 1839 for the design of the first stamp and, perhaps surprisingly, more than 2,600 entries were received. Prizes of £100 were paid to four people, but their entries were not in fact used.

11. *An entry submitted for the Treasury Competition by Robert W. Sievier.
From the Frank Staff collection*

Instead, a sketch by Rowland Hill was used as the basis of the famous Penny Black which was reproduced by the firm of Perkins, Bacon and Petch, whose founder was an American named Jacob Perkins. His firm were already experts as engravers of bank-notes and he had patented a scheme by which a stamp design could be accurately reproduced as many times as was wanted. The stamp was engraved by Mr. Frederick Heath. The design was multiplied by Perkins' patented process 240 times to form a complete printing plate.

44

12. *The Queen's Head for the famous Penny Black was taken from the Medal of 1837 designed by William Wyon*

13. *The Penny Black. The first adhesive postage stamp*

14. *A Mulready envelope cancelled with a Maltese Cross. It was addressed by Rowland Hill himself to an important G.P.O. official and signed by him (lower left). From the Frank Staff Collection.*

At the same time, a famous artist, William Mulready, R.A., designed envelopes and wrappers which, in the event, caused far more storm than the introduction of the adhesive postage stamp. To collectors they are known as "Mulreadys". The artist pictured Britannia sending winged angels to the various parts of the Empire. Although collectors find it hard to understand why, the temperament of the day was such that his envelopes met with ridicule. The stamps were an instant success. It is amusing to note the instructions printed on the sheet margins: "In wetting the back be careful not to remove the cement." It was not long before the authorities found that it was possible to remove the cancellation marks from the Penny Black and this led to the introduction of the famous Penny Reds which lasted for many years. The Penny Black —and the higher value, the 2d. blue—were imperforate, but the inconvenience to postal clerks was quickly recognized and experiments carried out to introduce a satisfactory system of perforation.

It would be wrong to suppose that the average Penny Black is a rare stamp. It is not. There were over 64 million of them printed. But it fetches a good price because, being the first postage adhesive stamp, it is probably the most popular among collectors throughout the world, and there is also a constant demand from specialists seeking examples printed by all the 11 plates used in their production.

Overnight, the introduction of the Penny Black pre-paid postage eliminated the complicated system the post office had set up for collecting and charging for mail.

The events that followed the introduction of the penny-post and the adhesive stamp were watched closely by the rest of the world and it was not long before other countries began issuing adhesive stamps.

In 1843 the Swiss cantons, Zurich and Geneva, issued stamps, in March and October respectively. In July, Brazil surprised the world by following Great Britain's lead with the famous "Bull's Eye" stamps. In 1845 the canton of Basle issued the "dove" stamp and, not to be out-done, the Postmaster of New York produced his own stamp. The now famous Lady McLeod local stamp appeared in Trinidad in 1847, and Mauritius became the first British Colony to issue stamps officially. The same year the United States followed suit. In 1848 Bermuda issued stamps, followed by Bavaria, Belgium and France in 1849.

By this time ten years had passed since the first adhesive stamp was issued, and from then on the number of countries issuing stamps increased rapidly until today every nation in the world uses postage stamps, and many regard stamps as an important part of their income.

In 1874 the General Postal Union came into being and a year later was renamed the Universal Postal Union. Today it regulates the interchange of mails between all countries of the world.

It was not long before stamps were used for a number of purposes additional to the normal delivery of mail. Here are some:

Air-mails

For some time markings and stamps, though not officially issued, were used on the early pigeon mails and experimental balloon mails which preceded the true air-mail. Most of these are extremely difficult to obtain. Then in 1917 Italy overprinted two Express stamps for experimental flights from Rome and Turin, Naples and Palermo. The following year, 1918, Austria organized the first international mail flights and from then on country after country began using special overprints for air-stamps and finally special air-stamps.

Charities

A number of European countries regularly issue charity stamps and most countries of the world have done so at one time or another. These stamps usually bear two values with a + sign between them. One is the postage rate and the other is the amount to be paid towards charity. Switzerland has issued its famous "Pro Juventute" stamps regularly each year since 1913. The profit from them goes to child welfare work. Funds, particularly in war time, are raised through issues for such charities as the Red Cross and War Orphans. In peace time, earthquakes and other national disasters are often followed by charity stamps to raise money for relief.

Commemorative

The authorities soon realized that stamps were a magnificent medium for propaganda. Countries began commemorating famous events or leaders in their history. Today some countries issue a stamp on almost any occasion—the opening of a public building, or the death centenary of a national or even a world-famous personality. Countries like Hungary and the United States issue commemorative stamps almost weekly.

SWITZERLAND

"PRO-JUVENTUTE"
1959 (1 DEC)

5c+5c   RECESS.   PRINTED AT BERNE.   NO WMK.   PIN.
REMAINDER   PHOTO. GRANITE PAPER.   PAINTED BY COURVOISIER.   NO WMK.   PIN.

"MARSH MARIGOLD"   "KARL HILTY"   "POPPY"
                   AFTER PHOTO IN SWISS NATIONAL
                   LIBRARY, BERNE

"NASTURTIUM"   "SWEET PEA"

1960 (1 DEC)

5c+5c   RECESS.   PRINTED AT BERNE MINT.   NO WMK.   PIN.
REMAINDER   PHOTO. GRANITE PAPER.   PAINTED BY COURVOISIER   NO WMK.   PIN.

2.—   1.—   3.—

"DANDELION"   "ALEXANDRE CALAME (PAINTER)"   "PHLOX"

4.   5.

"LARKSPUR"   "THORN APPLE"

SG 144-186. MINT.

15. (opposite) *Pro-Juventute charity stamps*

16. *Nobel prize-winners of 1901. Commemorative issued in 1961*

Postage Dues

Special stamps are issued for ensuring that the postal authority receives the full amount of payment. If a letter costing 6d. has only a 3d. stamp on it the Post Office attach a 6d. "postage due" stamp (twice the rate) which the receiver has to pay for or not receive the letter. This is perhaps the only field of philately left where design and production are not, so far, influenced by collectors. Consequently, most postage due stamps are plain in design and do not receive the attention they deserve from collectors. The postage due stamp is particularly interesting when it is an ordinary stamp specially overprinted. The most common overprints are the word "PORTO" and the letter "T" (for tax).

Locals

These are stamps issued in a specified area which carry no authority outside that area. Whereas a stamp issued by the British Government will take a letter to any part of the world (through international agreement with other countries via the U.P.U.), the local stamp would not be accepted even by its country of origin outside the area of issue. The field of "locals" is enormous and few countries have not, at one time or another, issued them. As the hobby of philately developed these "locals" ran on a par with normal issues. Then, for some reason, the major dealers, particularly Stanley Gibbons, dropped them and removed them from their catalogues. The effect was that fewer people collected "locals" for without catalogues they had no satisfactory way of valuing them. However, the "one-country" specialist, who naturally takes an interest in any "locals" concerning his speciality, has caused a strong revival of interest in "locals" today.

Certain "locals", such as the famous Trinidad "Lady McLeod" and the early locals of the United States, are still recognized by the main catalogues. This is because they were accepted by the government of their country of origin as necessary because, for instance, of a shortage of government stamps, or lack of a government service in the area. Among the best known are the Russian "Zemstvo" local stamps used by municipalities on postal routes which connected the localities with the trunk Imperial postal routes operating only between big towns.

17. *New York Postmaster's issue*

18. *Trinidad "Lady McLeod" local issue*

Provisionals

Sometimes a government is unable to provide the normal issues, and authorizes provisional issues, usually in the form of overprints. If, for example, a far-off island of the British Commonwealth suddenly finds itself short of 4d. stamps it may authorize 6d. stamps, of which it might have large stocks, to be overprinted to do duty at 4d. These issues have a fascinating interest to collectors for one very good reason. They come suddenly, and they are likely to disappear just as suddenly when stocks of the normal issue become available again. Therefore it often happens that the philatelic value of a provisional issue jumps steeply.

Officials

These are stamps intended for official government use. Normally they are the current general stamps overprinted with letters standing for the official service they represent, but in some instances special stamps have been designed for this postal duty. The first official stamp (never actually issued) was the 1840 Penny Black with the letters V and R in the top corners. Among British stamps the most common overprints found on officials are "I.R. Official" (Inland Revenue), "Army Official", "Admiralty Official" and "Govt. Parcels". The "Board of Education" and "R.H. Official" (Royal Household) are scarce.

Telegraph Stamps

These are not considered philatelic unless used for postal duty, as sometimes happens in emergencies. Many collectors argue that the telegraph stamp should enjoy a normal place in a stamp collection because it serves for the payment of a message sent by the post office. But this view is not accepted by the majority and it follows that anyone wishing to form a collection of telegraph stamps can do so at a fraction of the cost of normal postage stamps of equal rarity.

Fiscal stamps

Special stamps are printed for the purpose of tax payment on official documents, stamp duty, etc. These are not accepted by philatelists except as a side-line. But it happens that, as many postage stamps are used for fiscal payments, it is possible to have a postage stamp worth £5 because it is franked on a letter, and the same type of stamp, cancelled by ink on a document, worth a few pence, or, according to some philatelists, nothing at all!

This means that the collector must always pay attention to the cancellation of a stamp, which in these cases, can be very complicated. Some postage stamps bearing a signature appear to have been fiscally used when, in reality, the signature makes it a great rarity—a hand-cancellation made by a particular postmaster or clerk. Similarly, some fiscal stamps designed for fiscal duty and, therefore, easily identifiable from postage stamps, have been used on postal service. Known as postal-fiscals, they have usually been used during an emergency and are often worth a great deal. It follows that fiscals should never be thrown away without a good look at the cancellation!

Express Stamps

Some countries, particularly the United States, have issued stamps for special delivery, with designs or wording appropriate to speed delivery.

Newspaper Stamps

Although these started out, as in Austria, as tax labels (Imperial Journal stamps), they soon became postage stamps specially designed for newspapers. Many of the early newspaper stamps fetch fantastic prices (more than £2,500 in the case of Austria).

War-tax stamps

Wars are expensive and stamps were one of the methods used to raise money. Sometimes a country would simply raise its postal charge but, more commonly, stamps would be overprinted with wording such as "War Tax", so that the luckless purchaser might know the increased charge was only for the duration of hostilities.

Stamps as currency

Stamps have also been used for all sorts of odd occasions. Quite a few countries, such as Russia and South Africa (during the Boer War), have used stamps as "Emergency Currency". Some Russian stamps bore an overprint on the reverse stating that they could be used as coin of a certain value. United States stamps were declared legal tender during emergencies such as the Civil War, and for this purpose patented containers were produced to hold such stamps and keep them in good condition while serving as currency. Special emergency money was also created in the United States during the Civil War by incorporating stamp designs in small bank notes. The first issues of these were actually perforated.

Governments have also found themselves in difficulty when they have had plenty of paper money but too few stamps due to a shortage of printing paper. In such cases it is possible to find stamps printed on all sorts of items, including maps and banknotes. It is possible to collect complete banknotes used in Latvia, perforated and printed on the plain side with stamps. Similarly, Latvia printed its first issue (in 1918) on the back of German military maps used in the 1914–18 war.

19. (a) *A Royal Visit commemorative stamp of Jordan*

(b) *Fiscal stamp (France)*

(c) *Military stamp (Bosnia and Herze-govina). It was also a charity stamp depicting the Archduke Ferdinand, whose assassination precipitated World War I, and was issued to raise money as a fund for a memorial church at Sarajevo*

(d) *Newspaper stamp (United States)*

(e) *Airmail*

(f) *Official stamp. United States 1873*

Military stamps

These enjoy a popularity of their own, and form an enormous field for the collector. Apart from the large issues of special military stamps there are hundreds of military overprints. Armies sometimes put their names on stamps, e.g. B.E.F. (British Expeditionary Force), and to the collector of post-marks the military issues are probably the most fascinating of all. Envelopes also play an important part here as envelopes used by servicemen abroad are often sent at cheap rates. An envelope bearing a normal British 3d. stamp with the words "H.M. Ships Afloat" may have come from the Far East.

Essays

There are also a number of items, which although not intended for postal use, are avidly collected because of their close connection to the actual postage stamp. These are essays and proofs and are generally worth more than the definitive stamps they refer to.

Sometimes more interesting than the stamps themselves, are the essays which represent the designs submitted by artists for the issue, sometimes in large numbers, but not finally adopted. Many essays differ widely from the issued stamps. Others so nearly correspond that it is difficult, at first glance, to spot the difference.

Proofs

These are made from the stamp design chosen to show the issuing authorities what it will look like. Proofs may be of certain parts only—the frame, or the head of a monarch—or of the entire stamp, or the proof may be produced in various colours to permit a final choice being made (these are known to collectors as "colour-trials").

When the final choice has been made, many countries print a final proof which is sent to many individuals. In Great Britain, for example, final proofs are sent to the Queen and go into the Royal Collection. In countries like Austria these may be printed in quite large numbers.

Special stamps are also issued by some countries for mourning, plebiscite territories, mandate territories, occupation, pneumatic post and even farmers' parcels (Uruguay).

20. *An essay. A Treasury Competition design by Benjamin Cheverton, one of the four prize winners. Its actual size is a fraction over half an inch in diameter. The idea was to have these "stamps" embossed in rolls about 16 feet long, containing 240 stamps. The only examples known are a strip of four in the collection of H.M. The Queen and a single copy in the collection of Frank Staff.*

CHAPTER 4

COLLECTING STAMPS

A VARIETY of sources are open to the collector when it comes to obtaining stamps for his collection. Naturally the most satisfying source is the letters and parcels that arrive in the post for the collector and his friends. But restriction to this would mean that the collection had no system behind it. Nevertheless, it should be taken seriously if only to supply exchange material with which the collector can get the particular stamps he is seeking.

Through joining clubs and reading philatelic magazines which have columns devoted to people wishing to exchange, a lot of fun can be had "swapping" with other collectors. It can happen that a stamp badly wanted by one collector is not regarded very highly by another so a swap can be made to mutual satisfaction. Beginners who want to trade stamps with friends but are not quite sure of the relative values, could do worse than swap on a catalogue price basis.

In the past many magnificent finds have been made "in grand-father's attic"—even some of the great rarities have been discovered in this way. Those days are almost over. The world is stamp-conscious. Big business firms often keep the stamps from their mail to be sold to the philatelic world, and even the mail that has been kept for generations as mementos, has been recognized by most people as a potentially valuable possession and traded in.

Sooner or later the majority of collectors find they have to buy stamps to put their collection on the lines they want. It is for this reason that collectors pay so much attention to the value. They are not being mercenary when they say, "this is worth . . . and that is now worth twice what I gave." They have had to pay money for their stamps and simply endeavour to see that their collection becomes an investment as well as a source of pleasure.

The prime factor to remember about buying stamps is that buying a single stamp is always more expensive than buying in bulk. Stamps for a penny each can be had for less than a farthing when bought in packets. Although it may sound more expensive to buy in bulk it often turns out to be very much cheaper in the long run. Experienced philatelists, using their knowledge of stamps to advantage, will often pay a fairly large sum for a bundle of material merely to obtain one or two items. They then re-mount, write up and catalogue the remaining items and put them up for sale. It is not unknown for clever collectors to get more money for the re-sale than it cost them for the original material, several items of which they then have for no cost at all. No one would recommend a beginner to plunge in to the re-sale chances as it can be dangerous even for experts, but reselling on a small scale could be an interesting venture.

The beginner who is seeking a representative world collection, or wishes to acquire the stamps of the Commonwealth, or of a large country—philatelically speaking—like Great Britain, can certainly benefit from packet buying. Packet prices, in 1965, ranged from 5s. for 500 whole world different to 10,000 different for £16; British Empire 100 for 1s. 6d. to 5,000 for £38. It is possible to get very large packets of individual countries. In 1965, for example, dealers were quoting as follows: Tunisia, 400 for £5 10s.; Turkey, 1,000 for £9 10s.; United States, 300 for 21s. 6d.; Jugoslavia, 600 for 63s. Packets containing a good number of uncommon stamps can also be bought. Instances are: Portuguese Colonies, 3,000 for £65; Portugal, 800 for £24 and Spain 1,000 for £20. Packet dealers also cater for collectors of airmail stamps and thematics. A few examples of thematic packets commonly on sale during 1965 are: Flowers, 100 for 16s. 6d.; Music, 100 for 25s.; Railways, 100 for 13s. 9d.; Sport, 100 for 13s.; Ships, 100 for 11s. 6d. Expensive thematic packets like Sports and Games, 1,000 for £30 are also available.

The collector seeking to buy packets to form the basis of a collection can easily survey the market by reading two or three of the leading stamp magazines, such as *Stamp Weekly, The Stamp Magazine, Philatelic Magazine, Stamp Collecting* and *Gibbons' Stamp Monthly.* Any newsagent can provide a list of the various magazines available. Armed with several magazines the collector can see the widest range of packet material advertised by dealers at competitive prices—and as the prices vary considerably, it pays to study the advertisements carefully.

Another method of obtaining a basis for a collection is to buy a collection as such. Again, dealers compete with one another in offering country collections, subject collections and even general accumulations. Some of the larger philatelic dealers occasionally offer superb collections at prices in excess of £3,000, but some small collections can be picked up quite cheaply. Colonial country collections can be bought for as little as £4.

There is one danger to the collector who buys a formed collection advertised at a small figure compared to the catalogue value. Quite often it will be found that the collection has been thoroughly picked over by experts before ever coming on to the market. That means that the beginner has very little chance of finding anything of surprising value. Even so, he can profit from buying a country collection because it would cost very much more to buy the stamps individually.

The collector who specializes has greater advantages in purchasing material. Bank lots, Mission lots and Country lots are good hunting grounds and are usually sold by weight. One of the main advantages to collectors of these lots is that they are usually offered for sale by non-collectors—people who have little knowledge of the likely varieties etc. Banks, Missions and large firms often save the stamps that come in on their business mail: and these are torn off letters and sold as lots. Although these contain much duplication—which seldom appeals to general collectors—they are excellent sorting ground for the collector interested in postmarks and varieties, and are invaluable to the "plater". Some of these bulk offers are guaranteed by the Mission or even by the Government to be sealed and unsorted. This means that the dealer has not been through the stamps and that there is a sporting chance for the collector to find some good material—especially if the lot was sealed by non-philatelic organizations.

It is reckoned that there are about 2,000 stamps to the lb. When packed on the Continent, this type of material is known as Kiloware (in bags of 2·2 lb.) and usually contains good selections. Stamps purchased in this way are "on paper" and this makes them cheaper to buy because no one has had to spend time removing them from their pieces of torn covers.

To some extent, however, the collector is buying blind in all the buying methods mentioned so far. The advantage is that dealers have not got time to sort carefully through packet material. Nor does it worry them if a collector picks up a stamp worth £5 in a packet costing £1 because he will probably go back for more and tell his collector friends about it, bringing in more customers, and, in any case, the dealer bases his selling price on the cost to him, so he did not pay extra for the scarce stamp!

The collector can also have the advantage of buying stamps in his home and on approval. Hundreds of English dealers advertise approval services and send large amounts all over the world. Gibbons alone has been known to have around £250,000 worth of stamps out on approval at the same time.

Competition between dealers is such that many offer complete sets of stamps free to anyone who writes for their approvals. Quite a large percentage of these turn out to be cancelled-to-order stamps and generally is it not wise to be influenced by such offers.

The enormous advantage to the collector using an approval service is that he can ask for quite specialized sections and examine the stamps at his leisure. Naturally dealers sending out rare stamps on approval ask for references, but once these are supplied any collector can study hundreds of pounds' worth of stamps in his own home.

As well as providing an approval service whereby a collector can ask for a "book" on Great Britain, Queen Victoria or even Penny Blacks, some dealers sell in bulk on approval. Some services circulate boxes containing as many as 10,000 stamps at, say, fifteen for a shilling.

One of the most enjoyable ways of buying—or selling—stamps is through club booklets. Nearly all the larger towns and a good many small ones in Great Britain have a stamp club. Part of their service to members is to provide a packet of booklets containing members' exchange stamps. The parcel is sent from member to member until it has gone round the entire club, and the larger clubs are able to maintain a steady flow of packets. This is but one reason why any serious collector or enthusiast simply must join the nearest club.

The club member selling stamps is a greater potential source of bargains than a dealer!—if the buyer knows what he is doing. For one thing, the seller is not in it for a living and does not have to make a profit, and for another he may not know what he is doing anyway. A specialist in the Bahamas may not have any knowledge of Liberia, nor pretend to have. So if he is selling Liberia he may well let some bargains go.

Naturally it works two ways. He may price up his stamps far higher than a dealer would, as well as under-price them, but if the buyer takes care he can get some nice little bargains through club books. It also happens that a club member may have been plating a certain stamp, and finding himself with superfluous copies sends them round the club as plating copies at low rates. When the booklets have gone the rounds he may send them round a second time at a still further reduced price to clear them. This can lead to some stamps being sold at prices very much below the normal dealer's price.

The great danger of club-booklet buying is that collectors are apt, consciously or unconsciously, to put in damaged stamps: whereas a dealer, wishing to keep his reputation, makes sure that what he sells is first-class: or club members may offer stamps in the wrong classification, which trained dealers seldom do.

All in all, the collector can have a lot of fun going through club booklets and the fact that they are exceptionally good hunting ground for bargains is shown by the number of dealers who subscribe to the clubs just to have a look at the books! Many a dealer has bought a club booklet stamp for 3d. and sold it for 10s. because the first vendor did not know it was a "retouch".

The dealer meets the collector on even terms in yet another method of obtaining stamps—via the auction room. Here they compete in earnest for some of the world's rarities when they come on the market. Again it is a good field for buying stamps, provided the collector is fairly knowledgeable. It is far too easy at an auction to get the "fever", bid for something not really wanted, or bid more than originally intended.

Those without the time or wish to attend an auction room can bid by post and some auctions are conducted entirely in this way. Provided such auctions are run honestly they can be enjoyable and rewarding hunting grounds.

Collectors often find that the quest for stamps leads to pleasant relations with people of similar interests throughout the world. Some magazines give lists of collectors wishing to correspond with others, and soon an interesting exchange system can be built up. The specialist in an individual country does well to establish contacts in that country, and can often get material at little cost.

The more people who know you are a collector the better. Attending club meetings is valuable for this reason as well as for the social enjoyment that such meetings bring. You will soon find that collectors keep an eye open for stamps that interest their fellow collectors.

Expert Committees

Sooner or later every collector comes up against the problem of a stamp that could be extremely rare. More often than not it turns out to be a forgery or a reprint—that is why the genuine ones are rare. Organizations exist to help collectors wishing to check the genuineness of such stamps. These are known as Expert Committees and the better-known ones in England belong to the Royal Philatelic Society and the British Philatelic Association.

The committees are made up of the country's leading experts. They issue certificates stating that in their opinion a stamp is genuine and such a certificate is accepted universally among collectors. Certificates are made out in duplicate, one copy being filed by the committee, and the stamp is photographed in such a way that it would be impossible to use that certificate in conjunction with any stamp but the one submitted to the committeee.

It must be pointed out that on rare occasions specialists have ignored an expert committee's opinion that a certain stamp is not genuine and paid high prices for it, backing their knowledge against that of the committee. But this happens very seldom. The committees have at their disposal the most comprehensive reference collections in the world so that they can often compare a stamp sent to them with hundreds of similar ones, even though it is very rare. Their problem arises when semi-unique stamps appear and their opinion must be given without being able to make a number of comparisons. However, these committees are invaluable to the collector who makes a find. Their charges are related to the value of the stamp concerned, and render such a certificate well worth having.

CHAPTER 5

COLLECTOR'S EQUIPMENT

THERE are so many stamp collectors in the world that the commercial choice of accessories for the hobby is the most varied for any hobby. To deal with the key items first, we shall now consider the choice of album.

ALBUMS

In choosing an album, an essential part of a collector's equipment, the collector must first decide what type of collection he is going to form. Many enthusiasts do not want to take the hobby too seriously and are content with "one of each" of one or more countries. Perhaps the most common collection of this kind is that of the stamps of Great Britain, her Colonies and Commonwealth. For such a collection there are special albums beautifully produced—sometimes in two volumes—which contain marked spaces for each stamp and where the designs of stamps are illustrated to make identification easier.

Few people try to collect stamps from the whole world these days because any attempt at completeness would be beyond the means of the vast majority of collectors. But if a newcomer to the hobby cannot decide in what sphere to collect then he must sample issues from every country until he can form a preference. There are many albums which can accommodate such a collection.

Most stamp collectors select a group of countries like the West Indies or Scandinavia, or just one country. The advantage of this sort of collecting is that the compiler has a fair chance of getting to know a lot about the particular area and of being able to use that knowledge to advantage in obtaining stamps from dealers.

There are printed albums for a great many individual countries now. Some are very expensive but some, because of their popularity, like the specialized albums for Great Britain, are fairly cheap. It is usually found that purveyors of such albums provide additional printed leaves to cover new issues as they appear.

Enjoyable collections can be formed in this way with a minimum amount of trouble, but there are restrictions which are unacceptable to most senior philatelists. There is little or no room in such albums for blocks of stamps, covers, plate flaws and varieties all of which give the collector so much enjoyment, and the lay-out of the pages is pre-determined.

To overcome this many collectors use plain loose-leaf albums. This gives them complete freedom in choice of stamps and method of insertion. The world's most important collections are housed in this type of album.

The variety of loose-leaf albums is tremendous, but there are three main types. The least expensive is the spring-back, in which strong springs in the binding of the covers enable them to be pulled backwards to release the leaves or hold them securely, as you require.

The bulk of loose-leaf albums work on this excellent spring-back system which has, however, one minor snag, because when looking through the album one cannot lay it down open and flat. An alternative is one of the albums on the peg principle, in which the leaves are threaded on to pegs.

Another type is the multiple-ring album which may also be opened flat but which does not allow the leaves to be turned so freely.

If a beginner asks a philatelist what sort of album he suggests, the specialist almost invariably recommends a loose-leaf type. Whether it is spring-back, peg-fitting or multiple-ring is not so important, provided the owner takes care of the album and treats it with respect.

The advantage of the loose-leaf album over its rivals is that the collector can change the position of pages, take them out and add to them.

Leaves

Just as important as the choice of album is the choice of album leaves. When examining leaves the beginner must consider what qualities he is looking for. They should not, for instance:

Buckle and crease when turned
Act like blotting paper when written on
Tear easily

Many cheap leaves do all these things. On the other hand there is no special advantage in buying some of the lavish hand-made album leaves. The majority of album leaves are white but a number of collectors like to use black leaves, which can be very effective for some collections.

What the collector wants is a page that looks nice, is strong, and will not tear. Many spring-back and peg-fitting albums are provided with specially-constructed linen-hinged leaves to give added strength and ensure that the page is flat when the album is opened. One can also get transparent leaves to interleave the pages, or leaves to which the transparent paper is actually attached. Both afford extra protection to the stamps.

Mounts

There is no better advice than always to use the very best stamp-hinges available. The object is to use the least amount of hinge on a stamp compatible with maximum adhesion between hinge and album. Stamps must be secure, but good hinges will peel off the back of a stamp, when dry, without causing damage if they are properly mounted in the first place. A hinge should not be taken off a stamp while still wet: always let it dry first. Quality in hinges is worth a premium to any collector. As well as hinges there are also the Hawid strips which have a black background faced with crystal diamente which can be cut to suit the size of the stamp. Many find these are much preferable to hinges, particularly for mint stamps. But they are very expensive compared with hinges, and their use can mean that the method of mounting a stamp costs more than the stamp itself!

"Pochettes" have been superseded by these strips, which form a more efficient mount and also allow quick inspection of the actual stamp. Many international philatelic exhibitions have refused to allow pochetted stamps in competitive displays because they cannot be readily examined.

Covers and stamps on paper (kept like that to show the full postmark) can be mounted with the transparent corners used to insert photographs in albums.

Some stamps, such as the early embossed issues, require very delicate treatment in mounting. To avoid flattening the embossed surface they can be protected by frames cut from cardboard.

It sometimes happens that a collector will want to mount a complete sheet of stamps much larger than the size of the album. There are ways of mounting such a sheet and many collectors do so, but it does mean that the sheet must be folded, often more than once. If a sheet is worth keeping intact it is also worth keeping unfolded, and the best thing to do is to mount it on card slightly larger than the size of the sheet and form a separate album or folder.

21. *North Cape stamps of Norway—only on sale at the North Cape—the funds raised by these stamps paid for the roadway to the top of the Cape*

FURTHER STAMP COLLECTING EQUIPMENT

Tweezers

There are many kinds of stamp-tweezers about and there are only two factors of importance regarding them. The tweezers should be non-rusting and they should not be sharp. Tweezers may often be used to take stamps out of water (when soaking stamps off paper) or while hinging where moisture is met with. For these reasons it is important that tweezers do not rust. If they are sharp or have jagged edges they will damage stamps. Do not hold the stamp too strongly; use only sufficient strength to hold it securely. Some collectors do not use

E   65

tweezers and handle stamps very delicately. There is no doubt that an expert can "get away with it": there is also no doubt that if enough people handle a stamp it will be damaged. To avoid risk, use tweezers.

It may be said that the album, mounts and tweezers are essential items of a collector's equipment. There is one other item without which no serious collection can be formed and that is the catalogue.

Catalogues

The standard reference catalogues for collectors in Great Britain and the Commonwealth are those issued by Stanley Gibbons who, in 1965, celebrated the centenary of their first catalogue. They issue a giant Simplified Catalogue which caters for the main issues of the world. Then they issue annually three, more detailed, volumes, dealing with the British Commonwealth; Europe and colonies; and America, Asia and Africa.

The "S.G." number is universally recognized as a means of identification and, where a foreign country is holding an auction and uses other catalogues, it often quotes the S.G. number as well, because so many collectors the world over use the Gibbons catalogues.

Other important standard whole-world catalogues include: Scott's of the U.S.A., Michel's of West Germany, Minkus (U.S.A.), Yvert Tellier (France), and Zumstein (published in Switzerland, but only covering European stamps).

For the specialist there are often catalogues that deal far more thoroughly with particular groups of stamps than do the standard catalogues. So a collector who specializes in one country would need, if available, any specialized catalogues of that country. In some cases there are catalogues dealing with individual sets, listing hundreds of varieties that other collectors have established as regular. Such catalogues often reflect the life-work of a particular collector. Many of these will be advertised by dealers but some of the more highly specialized catalogues may only be obtainable through the specialist societies, are often printed in limited numbers, and can be very expensive.

The value of a catalogue to a beginner is that he can find out from it what a particular stamp is, when it was issued, how many other stamps there are in the set, and a general idea of the value of the stamp to other collectors. It must be realized that a catalogue value is the price at which that particular dealer is prepared to sell the stamp.

The value of a stamp is really what another collector will give for it. The dealer has his staff and shop costs to meet, so the price he wants is sometimes higher than one could get from a fellow-collector.

Prices change as they do on the Stock Exchange, and usually upwards. Whereas it is sometimes possible to buy a stamp at an eighth or a quarter of catalogue value there are also times when dealers advertise to buy stamps at more than the catalogue value. So catalogue values should be regarded as the dealer's price and as a general guide. Naturally the dealer who produces the catalogue must keep his prices within the general range of those of fellow dealers or he is likely to go out of business!

A word of caution is necessary here. It often happens that stamps described as "quarter cat." (meaning that the price is one quarter of the catalogue value) are not in the condition that the catalogue value is quoting, and that the stamp in that condition could be bought even cheaper than "quarter cat." from the dealer whose catalogue is used.

With the items of equipment already mentioned an interesting collection can be formed, but the collector who wishes to go into the hobby more deeply should consider the additional aids listed below.

Stock albums

These are produced in various sizes from very small pocket books to giant albums that will house many thousands of stamps. They consist, in principle, of pages of card, unbendable under normal pressures, and containing strips of cellophane or acetate fixed to the page at the sides and bottom of the strip, but open at the top. Stamps can then be slid into the strip and overlap each other. Dealers use stock-albums a lot; most serious collectors carry a pocket stock-book to protect new acquisitions and have a larger stock-album to house stamps that are waiting to be mounted in the collection proper.

Perforation gauges

A Frenchman, Dr. Le Grand, introduced the perforation gauge about 1866. Its use is based on the calculation of the number of holes in a fixed length of two centimetres. There are two main types, the gauge with the holes marked in lines so that a stamp may be "fitted" over them to see which row of holes fits correctly; and the gauge with converging lines which can be run up and down a stamp until the lines pass directly through the centre of the holes or the teeth. The latter is generally preferred. Being transparent, it can be used on the pages of a stamp album without removing the stamps at all, and further it provides measurement accurate to a decimal point. So when the collector sees "Perf. 16" it means that there are sixteen holes in two centimetres of the stamp's edge and, when he sees "Perf. 14 × 16", it means that the number of holes in two centimetres differs in the horizontal and vertical edges of the stamp.

Magnifying glasses

Essential equipment for those searching for flaws or wishing to measure gauges very accurately. Any magnifying glass is better than none, but several glasses have been produced specially for the stamp collector and are usually to be preferred. Some of the more up-to-date magnifying glasses used by collectors are illuminated, incorporating a torch bulb and battery to throw light directly on to the stamp to be examined.

Watermark detectors

The simple watermark detector consists of a polished black tile on which the stamp is placed face downwards. But the beginner should only use a watermark detector when all else has failed. The majority of watermarks can be seen if the stamp is held up to the light and looked through, or placed face downwards on a black surface. If these methods fail it is necessary to use a chemical such as benzine or carbon tetrachloride on the stamp in the special tray which is usually just large enough in size to accommodate a block of four normal stamps. In the vast majority of cases these chemicals applied to the stamp will show up a watermark or a trace of a watermark if one is there.

But the use of chemicals can be dangerous, not only to the stamp, but to the collector! Stamps printed by photogravure must not be immersed in these chemicals, and it is very dangerous to brush them with the chemicals though experts can get away with it sometimes. Both chemicals evaporate quickly. Benzine, the more usual chemical used, is a mixture of paraffin hydrocarbons made by distilling raw petroleum. It is considered safe on all stamps that are not photogravure, but it is highly inflammable. It does not affect gum. Carbon tetrachloride has a poisonous fume and should be treated with care. Where colours have been made from coal tar it can have a harmful effect on them.

There are also more expensive but safe electrically operated filter detectors. This type of watermark detector, through its filters, negatizes the colours on the stamp which then appears as a plain bit of paper enabling any watermark to be more clearly seen.

The humid box

Beginners can make their own humid boxes which are used for removing stamps from their backing. All that is needed is an air-tight, water-tight box. Put layers of blotting paper in the box and in the lid. Soak the bottom layers, but drain excess water out carefully. Then stamps on paper can be put in face upwards, the lid closed and the box left for ten minutes, or sometimes longer, to let the moisture work. Stamps should then literally slide off their paper attachments without the surface of the stamp getting wet at all. And, of course, any stamps with fugitive inks must not be allowed to get wet or the colours will run. Such a box can also be used to get heavy hinge marks off stamps. When taking a hinge off a stamp always remember to pull the hinge and not the stamp! Then, if anything tears, it will be the hinge and not the stamp. Stamps should be placed flat down when attempting to take a hinge off. If it does not appear to be coming off reasonably easily, use the humid box.

Most stamps can, in fact, be immersed in water and to do this a shallow tray is all that is needed. Care must be taken that the paper the stamps are attached to does not contain coloured ink markings that could run and thus spoil the stamps. A brush should be used to wipe the back of each stamp clean of gum traces etc.

Where a stamp is not affected by water, the water tray can also be used for cleaning a dirty stamp. If brushed carefully with water some of the dirt is likely to be safely removed. If this fails then benzine can be used. But remember that it is undesirable to have even water on stamps, let alone chemicals, which should always be a last resort. Folded or creased stamps should be wetted and then placed between dry blotting paper and "boned". Never use a hot iron; more often than not it will ruin the stamp.

It will not be long before the collector finds other types of equipment which, although not necessary for ordinary collectors, make things easier. They are mainly for specialists, but there are also such aids as transparent mending tapes for covers and roulette measures.

Library

One thing that most collectors, looking back, wish they had paid more attention to, is building up a library. A philatelic library becomes more and more valuable as the collector progresses, and out-of-print works often fetch surprising sums. Remember that many of these books are the result of years of research by other collectors and they make good ground-work for the newcomer to build on. It is, in fact, a good idea to keep all written material of philatelic interest because one day it may turn out to be useful.

CHAPTER 6

STAMP LAYOUT

WRITING-UP and arranging a stamp collection is one of the most enjoyable aspects of the hobby. It matters not whether the stamps on a particular page are worth many hundreds of pounds or a penny each; they can be attractively and interestingly displayed. A clean, well-mounted and properly laid-out collection is always worth more than an untidy conglomeration.

Above all, the written-up pages are the end-product of the collector. They represent his endeavours, his interests and his knowledge of philately.

The object of arranging and writing-up a collection is to display the stamps in the most attractive way. There are, in fact, no hard-and-fast rules for display and it may be said that displaying a stamp collection to catch the eye is in essence no different from laying out a page of a newspaper, magazine or advertisement. Vogues in lay-out, like hair-styles and clothes, change from time to time, and there is no reason why a philatelist should not try something new and experimental.

In the world of design and display there is a great deal of science. A page can be so clearly laid out that the human eye is almost sub-consciously drawn back to the point or points of interest every time it starts to wander off the page.

Most philatelic works are agreed that a simple lay-out is the best and safest. To achieve this there are two firm rules.

1. Make sure that the page is not over-crowded with stamps;
2. See that they are balanced.

When laying out stamps in several rows a simple rule is to try to prevent the finished page looking top-heavy, bottom-heavy or fat-centred.

There is no particular reason why a set of stamps should be mounted in order of denomination. Often there will be vertical and horizontal shapes which would make such a lay-out impossible to balance. In such cases, just lay the stamps out to please the eye.

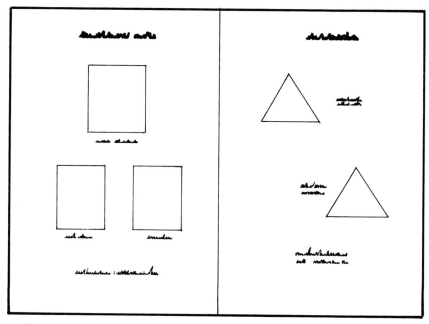

Well balanced pages need not have many stamps on them.

It is usually better to avoid putting used stamps on the same page as unused stamps, because the freshness of the mint stamps is marred by the postal markings on the used copies. Used stamps would not look unbalanced by themselves because they would be more or less equal to one another. Put them with mint and there is a conflict of neatness. However, where only one or two stamps are involved and the collector has them mint and used, then they can be arranged on the same page, using sufficient spacing—and this can give emphasis to the mint stamps.

Album pages usually have a quadrillé background. That is, the page is full of minute squares. So by counting the little squares the spacing and pattern of the lay-out can be easily and quickly worked out. It is good practice to try out several schemes before making up your mind. Once you have decided the lay-out you like best for that page, mark the positions of the stamps lightly with pencil on the album page. When the stamps have been mounted, the pencil markings can be rubbed out.

It is always better to keep one set together, either on a single page or on several according to its size, without mixing that set with another. But this is not a hard-and-fast rule and obviously, where an issue comprises a single stamp, there is every reason why other stamps should be put on the same page. But where it is not necessary to mix sets it is a good rule not to do it, especially if it means having one complete set and one part-set on a page.

With this simple and safe method, writing-up must be brief and to the point, in order not to distract too much attention from the stamps themselves. The customary details are: the name of the country, the date of issue, the reason for the issue, the watermark and the perforation. Do not jumble this information all together. Space it neatly in different lines; and balance the information with the lay-out of the stamps. Other information often put in is the name of the artist, engraver, printer, the type of paper and the number issued.

A sound rule is that which guides caption writers the world over; that a good caption should say something that the picture does not. The date of issue and the number issued is information not contained on the stamp; but the colour, unless it is a variety shade, and the denomination of the stamp speak for themselves.

Captions are subordinate to the stamps themselves and there is no reason for embellishment or flourished writing. Neatness is far more effective. Copper-plate writing can look very attractive and a variety of types of writing can be used, using special pen-nibs for the purpose. If your writing is not too legible, simply print the letters. Many collectors who cannot write neatly use a typewriter, a stencil set such as Uno or a transfer alphabet such as Letraset—though the latter is an expensive method. Those who favour a very simple write-up can buy gummed labels giving the names of countries, perforation and watermarks.

Although black Indian ink is probably used more than any other ink, there is no reason why a collection should not be written-up in a coloured ink such as green, red or blue. Collectors who favour black album leaves achieve a striking effect with white ink. But it is not a good practice to mix coloured inks on a page. If a page is being written-up in black ink and it has on the page a very rare perforation then the number of the perforation could be written in, say, red ink to draw attention to it. However, if the page is liberally sprinkled with red ink the effect of emphasis will be entirely lost.

Good lay-out is art and art involves taste. Today, the generous use of white spaces is favoured, as a glance at the magazine sections of national newspapers will prove. Such expanses of white are not found in pre-war magazines. The modern attitude is beginning to be reflected in stamp lay-out, as may be seen in the Centenary Souvenir Card commemorating Stanley Gibbons's catalogue exhibition at the Festival Hall, London, in February, 1965. The card, postcard size, contains coloured reproductions of eight stamps, see page 76.

Confronted by this unusual design, the eye travels automatically from the top two stamps to the beginning of the next line, travels along it and then drops to the lower stamp.

The collector who attempts this sort of lay-out as well as, or in preference to, the formal one can produce an interesting collection but, if it is not done well, he runs the risk of offending the eye instead of pleasing it.

Where there is a considerable amount of writing-up this can be used to balance with the stamps.

PLATE FLAWS
As catalogued by Heinz L. Gindl in
"Spezialkatalog Osterreich 2.Republik. 3 Auflage 1962"

1 Schilling green

25/I. White spot behind dot of "i" in
Osterreich and a black spot above
and slightly to the right.

80 Groschen red

10. Sleeve of right arm nearest edge
of design "open". Normally a line
joins the dark part of the design
across the white.

1.50 Schilling, blue

6/II Plate position - 76. Spot under
second "r" of Osterreich.

2/II Line through "b" of Republik.
This plate flaw is known to go
the full length of the stamp
with a spot by the left hand.

70 Groschen green

3/I Plate position - 9. Horn
protrusion from left forehead.

22. *A page of plate flaws, mounted in Hawid strip*

Within the image (part of the card):

British Stamps Current in 1865

Printed in 1965 for the
Stanley Gibbons Catalogue Centenary Exhibition
by Harrison & Sons Limited

23. The Stanley Gibbons Catalogue Centenary Card

Although it is a good rule to keep your write-up brief, there are many collectors who feel the need to put a lot of information on the page. This becomes almost unavoidable, anyway, when a collector specializes and goes in for research. There is no reason why a collector should not make his stamp album an historical and geographical account of the stamps as well as a stamp collection. But, generally speaking, if the writing-up overshadows the stamps and takes away their importance, the overall effect is spoiled.

There are several ways of meeting this problem half-way. One is to provide the extra information in an indexed addendum. Another is to interleave pages of stamps with information sheets. In this manner the pages containing the stamps make their full impact and anyone wishing to know more about them can read the facing page.

For those, like many specialists and thematic collectors, who want to write lots of information on the page containing stamps, it is important, as with the simple lay-out, to avoid overcrowding and preserve a balance between information and stamps. So if a thematic collector wants to write several hundred words about Mozart on a page, the easy solution is to put only one stamp on the page. In this way the solitary coloured shape will maintain its dominance over the block of written matter.

A reasonable exception to such lay-out is where a specialist is dealing with a set of stamps involving different perforations, watermarks, flaws and postmarks. It may be that hundreds of the same issue of stamps are going to be mounted. If the set is displayed first to set off its design, the subsequent pages can fairly give more attention to its varieties. The plate flaws and postmarks can then become more important than the actual stamp because that has already been displayed. Specially made philatelic arrows can be used to point to the actual flaws and drawings or photographs giving an enlargement of the area of the stamp being displayed, become useful additions even though they may detract from the effect of the stamp itself.

In the final analysis the collector must do what he wants and what gives him the most pleasure. If he does something unusual, something new, he is in step with progress, even if he sometimes fails.

If the art of displaying stamps is largely a matter of taste, the ways of mounting the actual stamps are not. The law of mounting is quite definite. Nothing must be done to damage the stamp. There are two principal methods. One is the use of the hinge, or stamp-mount, the other is to place the stamp in a pocket of some kind which can then be stuck in the album so that the stamp itself remains unstuck. The merits of these are discussed in Chapter 5 (page 64).

The vast majority of collectors use the stamp-mount, though some use pockets for very rare stamps and an increasing number of collectors of mint stamps use pocket strips. Expense is often a deciding factor and by far the cheaper method is the stamp-mount.

Hinging a stamp is very important indeed, because, apart from fixing the stamp to the page, the collector wants to mark it as little as possible and to be able to turn it over so that its back can be examined.

The general practice is to take the stamp-mount (gummed on one

---

Illustrations 24 and 25 (see overleaf)

24. *A page from the E. B. Ashton collection of Bermuda ship stamps*

25. *Research work. Here the plater has drawn the differences that enable the Bermuda ship stamps to be put into their correct positions on the plate. Some collectors spend a lifetime trying to plate a particular stamp. It is the perfection of specialization*

$\frac{1}{4}$d VALUE.

TWO PLATES WERE USED. PLATE I HAD ONLY A SHORT LIFE, FROM 26TH MARCH 1912 TO 1916 BY WHICH TIME IT WAS BADLY WORN.

PLATE II PRODUCED IN 1916 REMAINED IN USE UNTIL 1936.

PLATE I   THE OUTER FRAME LINE OF THE VALUE TABLET AT THE BOTTOM IS OF EVEN THICKNESS.

PLATE II   THE OUTER FRAME LINE OF THE VALUE TABLET AT THE BOTTOM IS THIN AT THE EXTREME LEFT.

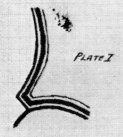

PLATE I

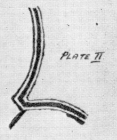

PLATE II

PLATE I   WMK. MULT CA ONLY   PERF 14 COMB.

43

55

NO 55   RETOUCH 3 LINES AT LEFT AND RIGHT ABOVE BERMUDA.
THIS SHOWS SECOND STATE. RETOUCH AT LEFT. VERY WORN.

SCRATCHES ON MOST STAMPS ASSIST PLATING.

IDENTIFICATION

PLATE 4

ROWS.

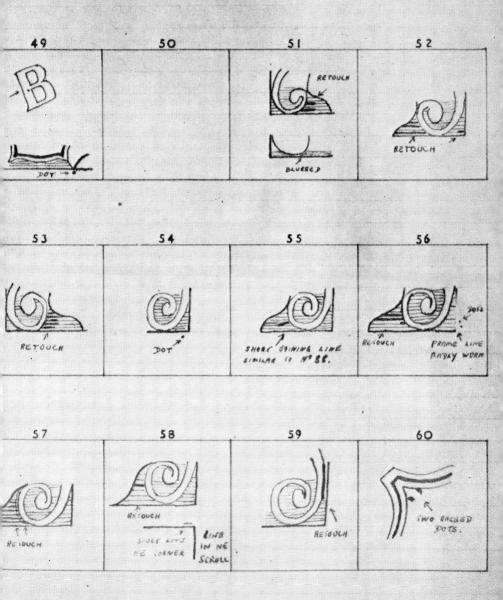

side only) and fold it once, so that a third of the gummed side can be stuck to the stamp, leaving two-thirds for the album page—and only part of the two-thirds should actually be stuck down. The mount should not be placed too close to the perforations of the stamp in case it is seen, and because if the rest of the mount was incorrectly applied to the page it might damage the perforations when someone lifted up the stamp to see the back. It is safer to place the hinge a tenth of an inch from the top of the stamp, and lick only the tip end of the remaining two-thirds of the mount before sticking it to the album page. This leaves the larger part of the hinge free and enables a collector to lift up a stamp and turn it over to examine the back.

It is important that the minimum moisture is applied to the hinge. Too much causes dampness at the edges of the hinge, either on the stamp back or on the page, and when the stamp is placed down the gum is likely to stick fast to the page and probably cause damage.

Many collectors, anxious to avoid such disaster, take even more trouble and divide the hinge into three parts so that they cannot possibly lick more than the edges of the folds. Those who have trouble getting the right amount of moisture on to a hinge often simply moisten their lower lip and touch the hinge to it.

The other system of mounting is to use the pockets or strips that avoid the necessity of sticking anything at all to the actual stamp. This is much more costly but, if done properly, gives a frame to the stamp which can be most attractive. Before the introduction of the black strips, collectors made transparent pockets for the stamps to fit in. The danger here is that in the course of time the pocket will slightly shrink, and damage the stamp, so that such pockets should be appreciably larger than the stamps they hold. Also if the wrong type of transparent material is used the chemicals in it can adversely affect the stamp, and it has been known for valuable stamps to be ruined in this way. But used properly this system of mounting can be effective and leaves mint stamps untouched.

The black Continental strips are more popular and would probably be widely used if cheaper. It could cost $\frac{1}{2}$d. to mount each stamp with this method. However, there is no doubt that it is very effective and efficient.

When an album is completed it is very important to make sure that it is kept at a reasonable temperature. Dampness or too much heat can cause damage. It is a very good practice to take an album out every month or so, turn every page so that mustiness is prevented, and examine a few stamps to see that nothing has affected them.

When handling stamps remember that while many people use their fingers very gently and carefully there is always a risk of damage caused by moisture or grease from the hands. Tweezers remove all risk, and experienced philatelists can use tweezers as nimbly as any fingers. (See Chapter 5 page 65.)

CHAPTER 7

THE COLLECTOR'S FIELD

DECIDING what to collect is one of the hardest decisions in philately because, to most collectors, practically the whole field is interesting. Because of the enormous number of stamps issued it is impracticable to attempt a world collection today, if there is to be any hope of completeness. The present-day collector is obliged to narrow his objective if he wants to form a worth-while collection.

Almost any aspect of philately has an interest and, if intelligently approached and treated with initiative, can become increasingly interesting. This is how new trends in collecting stamps are established. The research and efforts of collectors have revealed the fascinating new fields of philately which have quickly attracted other collectors.

When the hobby started one could comfortably collect stamps of the whole world, because there were not many to get anyway. Later on, collectors tended to prefer their own areas, Americans collecting America, Britons collecting British. This was all part of the patriotic climate of the early days, and a widespread if not universal attitude. Before the 1939 war, many collectors in Britain built up vast collections of Empire stamps and had little time for foreign issues—yet today the attitude to collecting is such that European stamps are fetching a greater percentage of catalogue value than the average British Empire stamps.

Two things may be said to have influenced collectors to take their choice from the whole world more widely than before. Cheap and easy travel has made these far-off lands more accessible and thus gives closer ties to them—secondly the stamp ceased to have mere utility value and has become a work of art illustrating every conceivable subject. Thus collectors with a particular religious interest would be attracted to those countries which commemorate religious events on stamps, while collectors with an eye to artistic design would concentrate on those countries which depict art on their stamps.

Perhaps the first great swing was towards French colonials which became a great field for the collector with a fancy for "pictorials". South America also attracted much attention until the reprints and cancelled-to-order stamps over-burdened the field.

By the end of World War II the enormous wealth of postage stamps available meant that collectors of Britain and the Commonwealth, or France and its colonies, were no longer true specialists. They were general collectors, but limiting themselves to a wide section of the whole field.

At this time the hobby had also developed so that experts had established themselves and the very construction of a stamp was traceable in detail. Some had devoted their entire attention to a single issue of stamps and their research work was becoming increasingly available to the general collector. Collectors were growing in numbers fast and prices—particularly for the early issues—began a steady rise which does not yet seem to have stopped.

More and more collectors began to specialize in a single country. Great Britain became a firm favourite for several reasons. It introduced the first postage stamp, its stamps are well designed and executed and— a very important point to most collectors—it has always played fair with the collector, never cheating him with reprints, never flooding him with unnecessary issues or remainders.

Serious collectors soon met a problem that had not worried the pioneers. The beautiful collections of "Chalon Heads" (a series of stamps bearing a portrait of the young Queen Victoria wearing her crown, taken from the full length coronation portrait painted by Alfred E. Chalon, R.A., in 1837 found on the early stamps of New Zealand, Bahamas, New Brunswick, Colony of Canada, Grenada, Natal and Queensland), which like collections

26. *The Chalon Head*

of "Penny Blacks", "First Issues" etc., were rapidly becoming too dear. So they looked round for a field of philately where prices were not so high, and investigated little-collected areas like Afghanistan, Siam and Turkey. The far-sighted collectors who picked the "unpopular" areas had a field-day. They unearthed facts and figures relating to their chosen areas that made fascinating philately; they studied hundreds and hundreds of dirt-cheap stamps to find rarities which, in the more popular countries, would fetch great prices because of their comparative scarcity. Then some of these collections began to come on the market. They revealed the interest of such areas, the range of varieties—and shortly the value of these stamps rose to meet the demand of new collectors influenced by the research and presentation of the originators.

Today there is no country without a philatelic following, and none from which an interesting collection of stamps cannot be formed.

Philatelists, like all collectors, are fascinated by the unusual, and thus alongside the "country" specialist we find collectors beginning to specialize in particular fields, such as the airmail stamp. The number of specialists in airmail stamps of the world, or of a particular area, grew so large that the prices of airmail stamps were often forced up although the numbers issued were greater than those of regular stamps fetching much less among collectors. It was simply that the demand had increased.

Serious collectors can no longer collect solely for the love of it, for values of early, and some modern, issues of almost every country are so high. Many would like to collect "Chalon heads" but are unable to spend hundreds of pounds on their hobby. True, there are studious collectors who pay for expensive material out of their philatelic profits, but not everybody wants or has the time to become such an expert.

The next trend in philately developed as the world's issues became more and more pictorial. Someone started specializing in stamps illustrating a particular subject, and this type of collection quickly caught on. For one thing, the value of the stamps was secondary and often a stamp bought for 1d. could say as much as another costing £50. For another, the "thematic" collection, as it is called, told a story and presented an attractive pictorial array.

Almost any subject can be illustrated by stamps, and among the more popular themes are flowers, animals, birds, Boy Scouts, the Red

84

ANIMALS BIRDS
AND
FISHES.

"FISH"
ICELAND

"CAMEL"
SUDAN.

"FISHES"
ICELAND

"KANGEROO"
AUSTRALIA

"TAPIR"
NORTH BORNEO.

"SHEEP"
SOMALILAND.

"KIWI"
NEW ZEALAND

"SPRINGBOK."
SOUTH AFRICA

"PIED FANTAIL"
NEW ZEALAND

"DAK BULLOCKS"
INDIA

"RAM"
ARGENTINE.

"SWAN"
WESTERN AUSTRALIA

"LEOPARD"
NYASALAND

Cross, ships and music. Thematic collections have won such rapid popularity that a number of books have been published dealing with individual subjects.

Not all collectors of thematics are satisfied with obtaining as many different "flowers" or "birds" as they can and simply arranging them with notes about the subject. Some have found more complex fields, such as history, rewarding. Interesting collections have been formed to illustrate historical incidents and figures like Christopher Columbus appear on the stamps of so many countries that hundreds can be found for a collection illustrating his life.

A history-by-stamps of the two World Wars would fill a whole series of albums. Stamps can even be used to trace the events which led to World War II, and propaganda stamps issued by all the participants have a close association with the war itself. Both the Germans and the British issued "stamps", not intended for postal use, lampooning the enemy leaders. With prisoner-of-war mail, military and other wartime mails the events of the war can be followed and official history corroborated.

One philatelic expert was able to alter the official history of the First World War. By specializing in Austrian Military covers he proved that a particular regiment had been in the field several months before the date given by the official history of the war. The evidence of some scores of letters written home by the Austrian soldiers and bearing the earlier dates was irrefutable.

Such thematic collections are often enhanced with material other than stamps, like photographs and documents, and can be made interesting even to the non-philatelist.

Perhaps one of the most popular thematic collections today deals with space. The first Russian space flights were quickly commemorated on stamps and each successive space flight by East or West has been followed by a deluge of stamps—from countries that have no connection with the events at all as well as by the countries concerned. The postal authorities of Russia were so highly organized that the day following their first astronaut's space walk, stamps were in the post depicting the incident.

A lot of collectors find great enjoyment in picking an unlikely subject and developing it through philately. Hence we find thematic collections of growing importance covering coins, ancient history and famous battles. For those who like thematics there is no subject that cannot be collected.

But thematics, although satisfying one's artistic urge and increasing the collectors' knowledge, do not content the probing mind of the person who wants to know everything about the actual stamps.

28. Space stamps, which today are one of the most popular forms of thematic collecting

It is not necessary that stamps should be worth a lot of money to be interesting. Nor is it always necessary that the actual stamp should be the most important part of the collection! Postmarks are getting the same attention as stamps today! Although for a long time the early cancellations were at a premium if they were unusual, the more modern ones were virtually disregarded. The only real attention given them was to see that they did not spoil the stamp, such as obliterations by "killer" postmarks. Then someone started collecting slogan postmarks, and this is now so popular that every post office issuing a new slogan-mark is besieged with letters from collectors enclosing the postage and asking for a specially light cancellation.

One pioneer of serious postmark collecting, Mr. R. K. Forster, set himself the task of collecting just one postmark from each town in the world—a "one of each" place-name collection. Now he has more than 50,000 different place-names, all carefully filed and tabulated. As there are well over 500,000 place-names he has a long way to go—but less venturesome collectors can have a lot of fun trying to get a "place-name" collection of one country; or even their home county.

The ordinary 3d. English stamp, so long the standard letter stamp, received considerable attention, and some collectors set about compiling a complete range of town-cancellation marks. Individually the stamps are worth little but a collection showing the cancellation of every post office in Great Britain is eagerly sought. Common stamps can also be collected by postmark dates—one stamp showing the postmark for each year that it was in use.

Interest in aspects of philately other than the actual stamp is so pronounced that many collectors specialize in the postal history of a period before postage stamps were invented.

The Mulready envelope, which appeared at the same time as the first adhesive stamps, and which was an alternative to them, was followed by satirical imitations which in themselves can make an interesting collection. Pictorial envelopes like the early caricatures of Great Britain and the Civil War propaganda covers of the United States also make a fascinating study. Postal stationery is also avidly collected and more and more countries are "playing" to the collector with ornate designs on their stationery.

Other collections can be made of control numbers, plate numbers, and the various attachments to stamps, which include advertisements. Until 1914 Belgium issued stamps with labels reading "Please do not deliver on Sunday". There are numerous oddities of this sort.

The most important thing to remember in selecting a field to collect is that the wise collector makes his choice in relation to the money he wants to spend and the number of stamps he desires. To most philatelists a collection of the Penny Black, Plate XI, would be both much too expensive and far too narrow a field of interest. By the same token a collection of the whole world would be much too wide a field. A happy medium is best.

Those who want to handle large numbers of stamps can select countries like Australia, United States, China, Russia, France or Great Britain.

The United States and France are better choices for the collector who likes pictorial stamps, who does not want to pay a lot for every acquisition and who wants a big collection. Both countries issue hundreds of pictorials at very cheap prices (and both also have their classics which can cost enormous sums). Those who like flaws and varieties can have a lot of fun with Great Britain and Australia.

The choice of collection is obviously a personal matter, but let us take a typical collector's field—the one country collection—and examine the possibilities.

Mr. X. chooses Austria. With well over a 1,000 catalogued stamps there is a wealth of material. With first issues in 1850 there are plenty of classics, some in used condition for as little as 1s. 6d. and some catalogued at £500.

He can collect generally for the whole of Austria or he can divide his collection and give preference to a particular section. The classics, The Austro Hungarian Monarchy, the Republic with its mass of cheap material of the 1920s; the 1939–45 period; the post-war period, charity stamps, airstamps, newspaper stamps; Imperial Journal stamps, postage dues; military stamps, the Austrian occupation of other areas like Italy, Montenegro, Serbia, Roumania or Turkey.

By dividing his collection into sections he can concentrate on a particular one according to his wish to spend, leaving other sections for when he feels like a change.

If he has just won the pools he can try newspaper stamps, which are catalogued as high as £3,500. If he wants to spend in pounds he can try the very popular charity issues; if he wants to economize he can tackle the mass of material of the 1920s which can be bought in bulk for shillings.

As his collection progresses with various degrees of completion in each section, and perhaps total disregard of some, his preferences develop and his collection takes on the lines of his particular aptitudes and desires.

If his inclination is towards deeper specialization he can sub-divide his sections and include others. For example, the period 1939–45 can be divided for those issues of German stamps used in Austria and those issued in Austria or overprinted in Austria. The year 1945 alone will provide a specialist with a bulky album once he starts assembling the various emergency obliterations that the Russian authorities ordered for every head of Hitler. He can add first-day covers, balloon mail, rocket mail, pigeon mail and the host of airline first-flight covers, along with essays, proofs, colour trials and black prints issued in advance of the actual stamps. Or, to go a step further, military stamps and postal history can be divided almost indefinitely to illustrate regiments or field posts.

29. *Austrian balloon cover*

Specialization can be carried to its ultimate. Mr. X, let us say, takes the costume set for his target. For this purpose the standard catalogues are hopelessly inadequate and specialist catalogues, available for some sets—as for this one, *Spezialkatalog Österreich 2. Republik* by Heinz L. Gindl—are invaluable.

Our collector finds that there are thirty-seven different stamps issued. Most can be collected with vertical ribbed gum, horizontally ribbed gum and flat gum. There were the 1948–52 issue, further issues in 1958 and yet another issue of certain values in 1964, all distinguishable by the paper used. There is an enormous range of shades and each stamp can be collected by date, indicated by a neat circular postmark showing each year of issue of each stamp. Slogan postmarks, commemorative postmarks and town postmarks can add volumes to such a specialist collection.

Then there are the blackprints, proofs, essays, colour trials and postal stationery of the set.

Even deeper specialization of the set is possible when Mr. X starts searching for varieties. There are different photogravure screens (70 and 100) and minute flaws on each stamp by which it can be assigned to its position on the original plate.

Mr. X buys the common stamps of the set (common now only in used condition!) in bulk. For a few pounds he can obtain many thousands. Armed with the catalogue and a magnifying glass he sorts through them for varieties and his remainder he re-sells as packet material at auction or to a dealer.

On the stamps he comes across a number of specks and marks not mentioned in the catalogue. They could be freaks with little philatelic value or they could be varieties. To find out—the hard way—he mounts each one and notes beside it what the unusual mark is. Then he compares each new stamp he comes across with them. If he can find two with exactly the same mark or preferably three or four, the stamp world will accept that he has established a hitherto unrecorded variety.

This is the fun of philately. As the years go by Mr. X reaps the benefits of selecting one country for his collection. His knowledge of Austrian stamps begins to out-run that of the average dealer who has to study the stamps of the whole world. He begins to pick up varieties that the sellers do not realize exist. The field is so wide that Mr. X can go on throughout his life—if he ever completes the costume set he simply starts on another. His collection becomes complete, but only by degrees. He may have a complete collection of every stamp issued but he can go on forever in pursuit of varieties and postmarks.

The same applies to forming a collection of any country. Many collectors prefer to take a stamp—perhaps an ordinary issue of Great

Britain—not already treated by specialist catalogues, and themselves start from scratch and find the minute differences that set one stamp apart from another. Although many philatelists regard this sort of collecting as narrow, it is not so when part of a general collection of a particular country.

The most dangerous period for a collector is when, after a few years of specialization in one country or area, he is tempted to give it up for some other country. This is usually the result of seeing a particularly fine collection owned by someone else. The temptation should be avoided because, if yielded to, it will only cause further temptations in a few years' time. Every area of philately has its fascination, so having made a choice and followed it for some time the collector might as well keep to it. Many collectors succumb, and chop and change; but those who resist are invariably glad—and their collections are usually much more comprehensive and interesting as a result.

CHAPTER 8

POSTAL HISTORY

L ONG before the appearance of the first adhesive postage stamp in 1840, postal services were running efficiently and on a large scale throughout many parts of the world. Exactly when the post system was first organized is not known, but many collectors delve back into the past to study the romance of the post, and its evolution; and this leads them into collecting old prints, documents and letters as well! Markings were often put on letters and for some time ran concurrently with the adhesive stamp. Not surprisingly, many of these postal markings are catalogued and can form a fascinating collection of this "pre-adhesive" era.

Although much of postal history is also concerned with actual stamps, generally, the term postal history indicates an interest in pre-adhesive periods.

As Stanley Gibbons is the bible for postage adhesive stamps, so Robson Lowe's *The Encyclopaedia of British Empire Postage Stamps*, is the bible for postal historians. In this are listed the major handstruck marks of Great Britain, catalogued from as little as 2d. to many hundreds of pounds. Robson Lowe's work also deals with subjects like telegraph stamps, railways stamps, local stamps, postal stationery, and many other subjects not dealt with in normal catalogues.

The study of postal history does not require a stamp collection at all. It leads the collector into a magnitude of side-lines, collecting such items as letterweights, stamp boxes, posters, Acts of Parliament and maps.

Some collectors tell the story of the posts with prints and old photographs in conjunction with some of the actual covers of the time. Specialists take a country or even a district and trace the mail routes. Although perhaps not strictly stamp collecting, this approach has evoked such interest that it must be considered as part of philately.

One of the great attractions of a collection of postal history is the added interest of the letters themselves. Letters written, for example, by soldiers after the Battle of Waterloo, have a valuable historical interest apart from the postal markings and give the collector a link with the past.

For those who like it, many profitable hours can be spent in libraries, old book shops, and museum archives in search of postal history.

There are specialist societies for the postal historian and there are dealers who cater exclusively for the collector of postal history. Apart from old letters there is a multitude of items that come up for sale at reasonable prices. In London, Robson Lowe, who introduced postal history as a separate study, holds regular auctions of postal history generally including early adhesives on their original envelopes.

Collections can be made of prints of mail-coaches; the various types of letter-boxes, early ships that carried mail and a host of other related subjects.

The hunting grounds for this type of material are antique shops, bookshops and junk shops, as well as the auction rooms and dealers. Old letters are always worth a sort-through when the attic is cleared. A field-day can occur when a local solicitor clears out his office "attics" which may contain documents going back for hundreds of years.

Letter-weights are a fashionable hobby on their own and some of them are works of art. They deserve a place in a general collection of postal history. Also there are the letter weighing devices and the little counters used for weighing letters. Some of these are inscribed "The Post Office Letter Weight" and "For Rowland Hill's plan of Penny Postage"—referring to his plan to have letters carried for 1d. per half ounce, irrespective of distance, in Great Britain.

Although most collectors like to embellish their collections with these sort of items, generally they give preference to actual letters and the markings upon those letters. These handstruck stamps are usually divided into sections for ease of identification among collectors. First there are the General Post Stamps which can normally be quickly recognized by the word "PAID" or the words "Paid at . . . [name of place]" which appear on the great majority of them, indicating that the postage has been paid and the post office at which it was paid.

Then there are ship letter markings, probably the most popular among postal history collectors, and they usually have the words "SHIP LRE" (ship letter) on them and the name of the port at which the letters were handed over to the post office.

94

Town, date and mileage stamps are another section. These show the date the letter was posted or the town, the route or transit post office. Mileage marks giving the distance of the place of posting from London (or Edinburgh or Dublin for Scottish and Irish letters) helped officials to assess the postage. An interesting aspect is the way the mileage altered as new roads provided shorter routes.

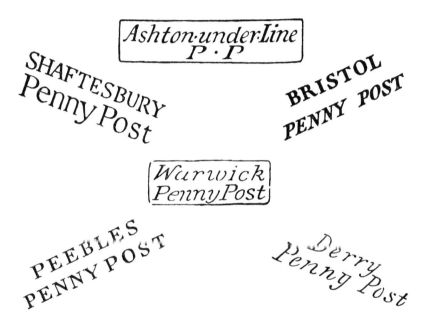

33. *Penny Post hand stamp markings, showing types in use from about 1812 to the 1830's. Usually found in red or black ink, sometimes in green and blue inks*

A popular specialist field is the franks. These were collected by autograph hunters long before philatelists came into their own. A frank indicates free postage, a privilege in days gone by reserved for special people. Members of Parliament had the right to send free mail. It is interesting to note that at one time the House of Lords rejected a bill because they were not included in it. Later both Houses were allowed to send free mail during Parliament sessions and for forty days before and after. Soldiers and sailors on active service were at times permitted to send letters at a penny rate. More often, service mail was carried at privileged low charges which were marked on the letters so that the recipients should not be charged the shortage. Letters of these bygone military periods are eagerly sought.

The great majority of these handstruck stamps are catalogued and therefore can be collected to a system by those who want to.

The envelope is another item of postal history though it runs into the period of adhesive stamps. However, the value of the early caricature envelopes far outweighs that of the stamps usually found on them. Until the Mulready envelope was introduced, letters were often just folded to make their own cover. Apart from the caricatures which lampooned William Mulready, R.A., idealists used the envelope as a means of propaganda. Elihu Burritt used them in 1849 to promote cheap postage across the ocean. Free traders, anti-slavery organizations, temperance organizations and Sunday labour propaganda make a wealth of material for collectors.

It does not take much imagination to see how a pre-adhesive letter

31. *A Mulready envelope caricature*

32. *Ocean Penny Postage propaganda envelope. Published by the League of Universal Brotherhood*

with its special handstruck marks can be written up and made interesting to people not in the least inclined to collecting themselves. For instance, a letter carried by one of Dummer's ships can be illustrated by all sorts of prints depicting the history of his services. Edward Dummer started a packet service in 1702 to the West Indies with the approval of the Post Office. These packets had a 95-day trip and, after ten of Dummer's ships had fallen prey to privateers or the French, and two to the weather, his service had to stop. But his pioneering was recognized and it was not long before the armed Post Office mail packet service was in full operation.

The study of airmails is also a concern of the postal historian for, though the aeroplane may be modern, airmail can be traced back to the ancient Greeks in so far as pigeons were used to convey messages of success at the Olympic Games to the major centres of Greece. The collector may not be able to collect the messages (he would be lucky if he could!) but, and this is one of the great joys of postal history, he can study the subject and unearth little-known facts to compile a collection of knowledge.

When Brutus besieged Anthony at Modene, Anthony is said to have organized a pigeon post between his besieged city and the relieving army. In 1280 the Tartars were defeated by the Egyptians largely due to their military intelligence—a pigeon post which as early as 1146 was used over ten routes in Egypt.

Attempts were made with swallows as late as 1854—without much success, but the collector comes into his own at the seige of Paris during the Franco-Prussian war, for messages still exist from the airmail pigeon service used by the besieged people. Messages were photographed, and reduced to 1/270th of their original size by a photographer, M. Blaise, which enabled many messages to be carried by one pigeon. During the seige, over 100,000 messages were sent in this way. The use of microscopic mail extends to more recent times—the 1939-45 war. Kodak Ltd. and the G.P.O. set up an airgraph service in 1940, and 16 mm. film was used in such a way that 1,700 messages could be carried on one roll! About 350 million airgraphs were sent before the service terminated at the end of the war. Another postal aspect of the seige of Paris was the use of balloons, some manned and some pilotless, to carry letters out of the beleaguered city. These are collected keenly and the history of each balloon trip is studied by French postal history collectors and air mail enthusiasts.

Little is known of the foundation of the posts in England and the postal historian can rummage as far back as the reign of King John to find information. For we know that King John kept a number of couriers to take his messages throughout the kingdom and that, by the reign of King Henry VIII, postal stations had been set up for the quick relay of mail. Official regulations for the post were brought in by Queen Elizabeth who also took the opportunity to prevent private posts without royal assent and thereby began the monopoly of the postal service. While, obviously, the collector can hardly hope to obtain early official documents, he can get photostat copies of those existing in the British Museum, the Post Office archives and the Public Records Office in London.

The first British Postmaster was Sir Brian Tuke, appointed early in the sixteenth century, and a print of his portrait can be found in many postal history collections. But the modern postal system began in 1635, under King Charles I, who granted Thomas Witherings a patent to open a postal service for private letters. Witherings created a system of weekly routes radiating from London to Bristol, Plymouth, Chester, and Yarmouth (which were covered once a week) and a service to Edinburgh—there and back—within six days. In that year, Parliament passed the first Postal Act which both emphasized the state monopoly of the post and laid down postal charges.

It was customary for the posts to be farmed out for rent, and in 1660 Henry Bishop paid a rent of £21,500 a year for the posts. Perhaps the most famous statement in philately was made by him in a letter dated August 2, 1661, "A stamp is invented . . ." It was a hand-stamp bearing the day of the month and was originally intended to guard against postmen taking longer than necessary to deliver the mail.

Henry Bishop is thus responsible for the first date stamp to be used on letters. The evidence for this, however, rests on a solitary document entitled "Answer of Henry Bishopp Esq., His Majesty's Postmaster General to some things objected against him . . ." The document is held at the Public Records Office and the relevant paragraph reads: "And a stamp is invented that is putt upon every Letter showing the day of the moneth that every Letter comes to the office so that no letter carrier may dare to detayne a Letter from Post to Post which before was usual." Henry Bishop's "stamp" was a date-mark and made no reference to the postage having been paid, or the amount to be collected.

William Dockwra is a name known to every student of postal history because, in 1680, this city merchant (in company with Robert Murray) set up a penny post service for the cities of London and Westminster and the inner suburbs with several deliveries daily. This worked so well that the Government suppressed it in 1682, and then ran it themselves! Letters passing through Dockwra's post were prepaid and actually marked "Penny Post Paid" with a triangular handstamp.

30. Dockwra's Penny Post stamps of 1680–1682

This mark was the first real British postage stamp even though it was not an adhesive.

In 1720 the postmaster of Bath, Ralph Allen, took over the cross-posts at a rent of £6,000 a year. The cross-posts connected towns by cross-country routes thus saving a journey to London and then outwards again to destinations which might only be a few miles as the crow flies. When he died in 1764 his efficient and well organised posts covered most of the country. Allen was a great postal reformer, as was John Palmer who greatly improved the conveyance of mail in Britain. The post-boys, many of them either teenagers or old men who carried the mail on a relay system, were easy prey for highwaymen. Nor was their job an easy one, as this official order shows: "This mail must be conveyed at the rate of six miles in the hour at least . . . And if any post-boy or rider conveying this mail is found loitering on the road, he will be committed to the House of Correction, and confined to hard labour for one month." Palmer suggested the fast mail coach and, despite strong opposition, was granted a trial between Bristol and Bath, to be undertaken at his own expense. The idea was that mail coaches would run to a strict time-table and their failure to arrive on time would result in quick inquiries about any mishap. Before then the mounted post-boys kept no time-table and would not be missed if they had been attacked.

On Monday August 2, 1784 the first coach made its run in sixteen hours, one hour less than the normal coach service. But although it was a huge success the postmasters were hostile, for the speed of the new service dislocated the organization of bye-and cross-country posts, and they now had to get up at night to receive mail-bags.

Nevertheless the Royal Mail coaches were adopted and given priority over all other vehicles. This led to a number of incidents, the most notable being the following: "I saw a great lark at Chatham. The soldiers were marching down the military road which crossed the main road. Traffic always stopped for the soldiers. The mail could not get through and Elwin, the guard, with whom I was sitting behind, insisted on the Queen's right. 'Damn the soldiers! Drive through them, Watson,' he cried to the coachman. So the coachman went for them and the soldiers had to give way midst a fair amount of bad language . . ."

Gentlemen's coaches sometimes indulged in races with the Royal

Mail, whose coachmen took up their challenge. This was stopped by the authorities, for a number of mails as well as gentlemen's coaches crashed off the road during such races.

It was illegal to obstruct the Royal Mails and posters, signed by offenders, would be put up as public apologies for such offences.

Specialist postal historians take a country like England or even a district and trace the mail routes, illustrating them with anything they can find relevant to the subject and often unearthing little-known facts that help to build up a composite picture to be handed on to other collectors.

Messenger systems were functioning in some parts of the world long before they did in England. Communication evolved naturally from the needs of kings and emperors. The rulers had to find out what was going on in their territories and, unless they knew fairly quickly, were likely to find they had been dispossessed. It is not always realized how highly organized the early courier system was. Clay tablets wrapped in an outer cover of clay were used by Babylon, and courier services were established in old China, Mexico and many other early civilizations.

To give an idea of the size of some of these organizations we may note that Marco Polo (though perhaps a rather gullible historian) recorded the Great Khan's postal service as employing 200,000 horses and some 10,000 buildings.

Some historians have credited Cyrus the Great with setting up the first relays. Certainly by Roman times there was an elaborate system, run with military precision, the couriers even bearing official identity badges, the tabellarius, with the letters SPQR standing for the authority of the Senate.

It is from the Romans that we take the word "Post" (positus) the name given to the stations where couriers handed over the mail or took fresh horses.

These early systems, however, did not benefit the public. If the leaders realized the necessity for quick communication they also perceived the desirability of preventing other people from finding out too much too quickly. The educated noblemen had to provide their own couriers and face the risks of losing them on the lawless frontiers of civilization.

When Rome fell the post collapsed except in the Eastern part of the

Empire. The centres of learning—monasteries and universities—took over and before long they introduced the private posts by taking other people's mail for a fee. Chinese merchants who let their couriers carry general mail found the call on their services so great that as early as the fifth century full-time mail-carrying organizations were set up.

These operated with success right up to the twentieth century when, following Europe's lead, the Chinese government closed them down and assumed a monopoly of the entire mail.

In France, Louis XI organized a very efficient postal service and took the great step of allowing the general public to use it. The fees charged, however, excluded all but noblemen, and even they had to agree to having their mail censored before it could be delivered by the Royal couriers.

The student of postal history will see quite clearly how the monarch built up fast and reliable services, but excluded the public from using them. Then, when many rivals appeared, the rulers decided to take over completely and have the benefit of controlling the mail and the revenue from it.

The word mail comes from the French "malle" meaning travelling bag and it is believed that the French set up the first post for the general public. Richelieu, Postmaster-General, devised a public postal system which catered for the entire public and even provided for a registered letter service.

Indeed, it seems possible that William Dockwra was inspired by a French local post operating in Paris in 1653, twenty-seven years before Dockwra launched his London post. The Parisian post was organized under royal patronage by a M. de Villayer whose customers had to enclose their letters in wrappers known as *billets de porte payé* and—this was a real innovation—post them in letter boxes from which they were collected. The de Villayer postman stripped the wrappers and then delivered the letters to the addressees. As a result, no wrappers are known to have survived, but postal historians consider that they must have borne some postal markings equivalent to a Dockwra "stamp".

But if France gives the collector his first slim chance of acquiring stamp markings, the Thurn and Taxis post yields the greatest romance. The Thurn and Taxis family entered the mail business as early as 1290 —probably earlier—when Omedio Tassis opened routes for the post in Italy. By 1450 they had extended the post from Bergamo to Vienna and thirty years later to Brussels. The family operated on behalf of royalty, but when Philip I of Austria did not keep his agreement with Francis von Taxis the family opened the service to the public. The public responded and the Thurn and Taxis post grew into the greatest service in Europe at that time. At one time their mail messengers covered Germany, Austria, Italy, the Netherlands, Belgium and Spain. By 1800 the family were taking more than a million florins a year.

Prussia took over the postal system in 1867, paying the family an indemnity of 3,000,000 thalers. Actual postage stamps of the family post exist from 1852 and are catalogued under Germany. This private postal system lasted for over 500 years and covered more than 25,000 square miles.

The development of mail services overseas was a more hazardous business because of the risks from piracy, privateers and weather. Ships' masters would deliver private as well as official mail. Some sailing ships calling at Cape Town would leave mail literally under large stones, to be picked up by the next homegoing ship. In Massachusetts Bay in 1638 ships' captains were the only agents for transporting mails and hung bags in local coffee houses and taverns so that mail could be put in them.

The scheme, however, proved unsatisfactory, and in 1639 the colonists authorized Richard Fairbanks to look after the incoming and outgoing mails.

The first attempt to organize a mail service between the American colonies ended in disaster. Francis Lovelace, Governor of New York in 1673, inaugurated the scheme by establishing a monthly mail service to Governor Winthrop of Massachusetts. But Red Indian war parties captured most of the mail.

Thomas Neale was granted the monopoly of American posts in 1692, and from then on the postal system gradually spread, but there were many complaints because of the lack of fixed charges and eventually the British Government acquired the postal rights for nearly £2,000, it is believed.

Among the great names of American postal history is that of Benjamin Franklin (1706–90) who apart from his postal reforms took part in the War of Independence, was elected president of Pennsylvania three times and figured prominently in public life. He organized the first house-deliveries in America and, incidentally, made the system profitable for the first time. Several scientific discoveries also stand to his credit. Franklin was arbitrarily sacked in 1774 because of his strong sympathy with the cause of American Independence.

It was not very surprising when he appeared again as a postal expert, this time for the Confederation. With him as Postmaster General, the new Continental Post Office interfered actively with the Royal Mail and made things so difficult that in 1775 the King's Postmaster ceased to function.

After the War of Independence had been won by the Americans, Samuel Osgood was made Postmaster General and found himself in command of a mere 75 post offices. As the network began to spread the postal authorities met with severe losses because many private express companies and carriers could deliver mail more cheaply and more quickly. In the early days of postage adhesive stamps these companies, notably the Pony Express, issued their own stamps.

Postal history is one of the few branches of philately where there is still a tremendous amount of research needed and collectors interested in this type of collecting can often tread virgin ground. Much of the English postal history has been written fully by Frank Staff (*The Penny Post 1680—1918*, and *The Transatlantic Mail*). The romance of the early mail carried over the sea before the days of steam has attracted much attention and many books have been published on this specialist subject. Outstanding in this field is the monumental work, *The Maritime Postal History of the British Isles*, published privately by its author, Alan W. Robertson. Less known and explored, at least by British philatelists, and waiting attention, is the Napoleonic mail which is still fairly easy to obtain. The Boer War, combining stamps and covers, offers a wide scope for those wanting more recent military history. In short, postal history provides an alternative to stamp collecting and is a subject of intense social and historical interest beyond philately.

34. *Boer War local post. Mafeking Siege stamp showing Cadet Sgt. Major Goodyear*

CHAPTER 9

BRITISH AND COMMONWEALTH STAMPS

As Great Britain led the way with adhesive postage stamps it was natural that her empire should follow and it is probably true to say that these stamps, together with those of the more recent Commonwealth, have been collected more thoroughly than those of any other nation—certainly in this country.

Specialist collections have been built up of every single country or island in the old Empire where stamps were issued. Collectors who do not want too much specialization have taken areas of the Commonwealth, such as Africa, West Indies, Australasia, all of which require a multitude of stamps to be collected to form a comprehensive collection.

A more recent method of collecting the Commonwealth is for the collector to pick a reign, such as Queen Elizabeth II, and try and complete it throughout the entire Commonwealth. Collections of this sort covering the reigns of King George VI and Elizabeth provide colourful and pictorial designs. So popular is this type of collection that Stanley Gibbons have produced a special catalogue, *Elizabethan Postage Stamp Catalogue*. It is significant too that the prices in this catalogue are in dollars as well as sterling! Already 5,500 stamps are listed for the reign of Elizabeth. There is also the *Commonwealth Catalogue of Queen Elizabeth II Stamps*, published by the Urch Harris and Co. Ltd. of Bristol.

As most of the definitive sets range from ½d. to £1 it can be an expensive field for the mint collector; but many collectors overcome this by collecting "short sets" up to 1s. value.

The Commonwealth also provides the new collector with a chance to start at the beginning! A number of states have, through independence, only recently come into existence, particularly in Africa. This means that there are no early stamps catalogued at many hundreds of pounds and the collector can perhaps buy the very first stamp of the country for 6d.

It is worth noting that of the new countries say five or six years old, their first issues have now all gone up in value; and collectors have all had the chance to get them on the new issue service. There is an added advantage in taking the stamps of a modern issue country in that the collector can study them carefully to find errors and flaws which may not reach the catalogues until much later.

But there is no need to be put off by a country because it contains stamps of very high value. British Guiana, for example, where there is no stamp under £55 on the first page of Stanley Gibbons catalogue, still offers the new collectors a wide range of stamps at reasonable prices. And some of the quite cheap modern issues have many interesting varieties.

Of course, Great Britain, is the most popular country of the Commonwealth stamp-issuing areas, and a large collection can be formed without even touching the early issues. After years of aloofness to the philatelic world it seems the Post Office is now paying attention to the need for pictorial designs.

In 1965 came the Churchill stamp issue, which has probably more flaws than any other modern English stamp! Then there have come commemorative issues on the 700th anniversary of Simon de Montfort's Parliament, Lister, Salvation Army, Battle of Britain—all in the space of a few months. In addition, Great Britain issued stamps, in common with most other countries for the centenary of the International Telecommunication Union and the twentieth anniversary of the United Nations. In June 1966, Britain issued its first stamps depicting sportsmen in action—commemorating the World Cup.

35. *The Battle of Britain fourpenny stamps. The first English commemorative stamps to be printed se-tenant*

Areas like British North America, Indian States, Africa and Australasia, provide a wealth of material. To give the new collector an idea of the potential field we will examine one of these areas—Australasia.

This is probably the finest area for a new collector because it offers something of everything and can be sub-divided into many small components or types collected for one huge collection.

He can start his collection with Australia proper which first issued stamps in January 1913. If he likes flaws, shades, perforations and watermarks, and so on, then he can fill albums with the first few issues, the Kangaroo stamp (framed in a map of Australia) and the King George V type stamp which was in use from December 1913 to 1930. Or he can form a straight collection of them based on catalogue numbers of just over a hundred stamps.

36. *Australian Diamond Jubilee stamp commemorating the first Australian air-mail*

Then come a series of particularly beautiful stamps, notably the opening of Parliament House, the Air stamp of 1929, the centenary of Western Australia, Kingsford Smith's flights, the Lyre-bird, Sydney Harbour Bridge, and the centenary of Victoria. The colours of some of these stamps are a lesson in perfection to many other countries.

In the reign of George VI Australia produced a profusion of stamps in different shapes and sizes and many of them at low catalogue prices.

The awakening of Australia to the world of art is expressed quite clearly on the modern issues where artists have been allowed considerable licence. The conventional stamp frame disappeared for some of these, like the Henry Lawson and the anniversary of the founding of U.P.U. stamps. The 1950 Aborigine stamp is considered by many to be one of the finest modern stamps. Elizabeth II stamps are no less beautiful with unusually good portrayals of the Queen (SG.94), the Mail Coach Pioneers issue showing a Cobb and Co. coach and the introduction of multi-coloured stamps.

Although Australia started its issues in 1913, stamps were issued in Australia very much earlier and the collector who wants early issues will still find the Victorian stamps of Australia the easiest to obtain. They were issued by the states of New South Wales, Queensland, South Australia, Tasmania, Victoria and Western Australia. Naturally a number of these are very rare but a large collection can be made of these states for little outlay—and the field offers the specialist opportunities for flaws and varieties. Some of these stamps, such as the Sydney views, early portrait types of New South Wales and the first swans of Western Australia, are among the classics and can be very costly, but hundreds of stamps from these states can still be acquired for 1d. to 6d. each.

37. *A freak from the Davidson Putwain collection caused by a piece of paper dropping on the plate during the printing*

The common "middle issues" of these states give a collector a good chance to pick up rarities if they have studied the stamps, for there are numerous varieties—and there is always a chance of finding them among the common stamps.

The collector can spread his field to include Papua, British New Guinea and New Guinea stamps which come under Australia, as well as Australian Antarctic Territory.

38. Australian stamps

Besides Australia, New Zealand is a popular specialist field. As early as 1898 New Zealand was issuing pictorial designs depicting Pembroke Peak, Lake Taupo, the Sacred Huia birds, and Lake Wakatipu.

The classics of New Zealand are the Chalon Heads and with nearly 150 listed by Stanley Gibbons, some can be obtained comparatively cheaply. It is in this range that the new collector will get to understand the importance of condition for he will see in catalogues prices ranging from 70s. to £28 and £8 to £60. Care has to be taken with some of the imperforate issues as it is not unknown for perforated stamps, otherwise the same, to have been scissor-cut to make them appear imperforate.

Early pictorials are felt by many to be undercatalogued today— perhaps a good thing for the collector. In this range too there are stamps, such as the 1d. Universal Penny Postage issue which can be made the subject of a collection in themselves. Stanley Gibbons list fifty-three different stamps of this one type.

New Zealand's Health stamps are famous in the world of philately and some of them have reached high catalogue value. On of the finest pictorial sets of New Zealand was issued in 1940—the centenary of proclamation of British sovereignty. The beautiful blue-green ½d.

showing the arrival of the Maoris in 1350, a common stamp is a striking example of art on stamps. Triangular stamps were issued in 1943 showing Princess Margaret and Princess Elizabeth.

New Zealand is also linked with some of the Pacific Islands, Rarotonga—or Cook Islands—Aitutaki, Niue, and Penrhyn islands.

Altogether the collector of Australasia has a field full of everything. Also of great interest is the postal history of the area.

One of the main advantages of being a collector of Commonwealth stamps is that just about every stamp club in the country has members who are fellow Commonwealth collectors. This enables the new collector to enjoy swapping sessions and pick up some useful tips.

Nevertheless, the most popular of all among the "British" stamps are those of Great Britain herself. Some idea of the following these stamps have can be derived from the fact that Stanley Gibbons introduced, in 1968, a special "Price List" of the Stamps of Great Britain, which acts as an effective catalogue. This booklet had to be reprinted three times in the same year! To provide a full introduction to this subject I have written a book entitled *The Stamps of Great Britain: A Beginner's Guide*, which will be published by Lutterworth Press in the Autumn of 1969.

CHAPTER 10

FORGERY

W E have already discussed cancelled-to-order stamps, reprints and bogus issues, but these are not really forgeries as they were not produced to deceive—though they may be used to deceive. Although such stamps start their life in their true colours they are often offered to collectois as originals and are not always easy to detect. In philately various terms are used to describe each type of forgery. These are:

Facsimile

A stamp that is an exact copy of the original but that has a mark on it, sometimes the word "facsimile", to show that it is a copy. These are usually detectable with an observant eye but dangers do arise when the mark has been carefully removed from the stamp.

Fictitious

A reproduction of a stamp for a purpose such as illustrating articles.

Postal Forgery

The real forgery is rare and, especially in genuine used condition, is often valuable. It is a stamp produced for the purpose of deceiving the postal authorities. There have been some very successful forgeries such as the 1871–72 shilling of Great Britain, used on telegrams, which escaped detection for a long time.

Philatelic Forgeries and Fakes

Philately uses these words to distinguish between forgeries to defraud the post office and those to defraud a collector. Books about such stamps were on sale as early as 1862, which shows that counterfeiters were early attracted to the field of philately. Fortunately, today, the collector with the right equipment can easily detect the vast majority of the early philatelic forgeries. Modern science has produced advanced methods of detection of which those early counterfeiters never dreamed.

Their modern counterpart, however, produces his wares with a view to cheating collectors. How successful he is only future generations will know. A perfect forgery remains undiscovered so, although we are aware of many forgeries, we do not know how many successful ones exist.

It is unlikely that there are many. The equipment necessary to produce such a perfect copy of a stamp is probably nearly as expensive as that required by the authorities. The skill required is such that only a handful of men could approach perfection, and the money they could earn from their talent makes it unlikely they would risk their freedom by forgery.

A stamp that began as a genuine issue, but has been tampered with is the real danger to the collector. Common fakes include stamps with changed colour, perforation and even value. In a set whose design is the same throughout, the less expensive denominations sometimes have the original value removed and replaced by a higher value.

In 1965 it was found that an unusually large number of early Norwegian stamps with ships' postmarks were appearing on the market, especially in German auctions. An examination revealed that a large number of these cancellations were forged and originated from a collector in Bodo, Norway. Before the end of 1965 experts like Mr. F. C. Moldenhauer, editor of Nordisk Filatelist Tiddskrift, had listed and dealt with these fake postmarks in such detail that they were able to tell the philatelic world that the forger had used illustrations on page 62 of the Norwegian Handbook as his guide!

A fake exists where a postmark is erased to make a stamp mint; where a rare postmark is added to a stamp; where an overprint is added, or where a common overprint is tampered with to make it a rare "error" overprint. If, for example, an overprint is rare without a full stop after the words, the counterfeiter with a genuine stamp and a genuine overprint has only to erase that single full stop to produce a rarity.

The experts combat such attempts with knowledge, experience, and scientific equipment, but are often unable to give more than an opinion. So it is no good trying to belittle the damage to philately done by the counterfeiter. The main protection of the ordinary collector is to know his source. If he buys a rare stamp of a type known to have been copied by counterfeiters he should buy it from a reputable dealer who will back it as genuine, or happens to have first-hand knowledge of the history of the stamp in question.

There are some really tough fakes. Sometimes a set has been produced officially both perforated and imperforate. If a compound perforation is worth much more than the imperforate, the counterfeiter need only buy an imperforate copy with four good margins and produce the compound perforation. Everything about the stamp is then perfectly genuine except the perforation.

Philatelists are perhaps lucky that the man who seeks to counterfeit invariably does so for profit. Therefore he is loathe to spend more than he needs on the product and is content, usually, to pass his wares off on the unwary collector. When experts examine them they will usually find something wrong. The methods of manufacture will often have changed, or the chemical make-up of the gum be no longer obtainable, or its method of spread on to the back of the stamp may not be that used at the time of the original stamp. To foil the expert the counterfeiter has not only to produce exactly what he sees in the original—at which he may be well skilled—he has also to be an expert philatelist and know the entire history of the manufacture of that stamp.

The true forgery is often worth very much more than the original stamp—especially if it is particularly well produced—and the collector has little to fear, financially, from this compared to the danger of fakes and reprints which often are worth only pennies whereas the originals may be catalogued in hundreds of pounds.

The classic British forgery, the Stock Exchange forgery, is worth a good deal more than the original stamp! It comes in the 1867–80 set of Victorian stamps and was made of Plate V, 1871 and Plate VI, 1872, of the shilling value. It was not until 1898 that the authorities realized it existed! All known copies of the forged stamps were found on tele-graph forms used at the Stock Exchange Telegraph Office. Yet many of them would not deceive a philatelist for very long. They were pro-duced on unwatermarked paper (the originals have Emblem water-marks) perforated 14 like the originals; but the check letters are blurred and have combinations that were not used by the authorities, including the letters after the "T" which was the last genuine letter used. The forgeries appear to have been issued in June and July of 1872.

A collector's main defence against forgery of any kind is to know that a forgery exists of the particular stamp he has. Once he is on his guard he can seek advice from experts. It is always worthwhile building up a collection of fakes and forgeries with which to compare later acquisitions.

A valuable stamp should always be examined with exceptional care, remembering that repairs may be invisible to the naked eye. Careful scanning with a powerful magnifying glass will reveal any traces of interference. It is not uncommon to find that stamps printed imperforate with magnificent margins have in fact got forged margins. An expert forger will patiently scrape down the original margins and graft on the larger margins, a process only detectable by a powerful glass.

Any uncatalogued colour shade should be suspected. In many cases such shades turn out to be nothing more than the effect of exposure to the elements during the letter's travels. Chemicals can change colours completely and forgers have used them to create "uncatalogued" shades and colours.

On some stamps it is fairly easy to remove the cancellation and quite simple to replace gum on the back of a stamp, though not so simple to replace the exact type of gum used on the originals. As some postmarks are very rare the faker will often replace the original postmark with a rare mark. This helps him to cover up his removal work and allows the back of the stamp to remain untouched. As many postmarks are rough or blurred his work is not too difficult.

Although stamps on cover afford some protection against faking, since they are more likely to be genuine, there are plenty of cases where faked stamps have been put on covers. A common stamp already on cover is removed and the rare one put in its place with the cancellation carefully worked to conform to that part of the cancellation actually on the cover.

A thinned stamp can be treated in the same way as the wide margin fakes. Extra paper is grafted on. This also applies where there is a hole in the stamp, and here the faker will go as far as to paint in the design of the stamp over the filled-in portion. There are some exceptionally good fakes of stamps which collectors think are great rarities, such as a pair of stamps "imperf between", i.e. where the two joined stamps are perforated round the edges but not where the two stamps are joined. In such cases the faker has obtained the normal pair and carefully grafted paper over the centre perforations, creating the desired rarity.

Just how rife forgery is we are not able to tell, as we only know about the ones that are found out. But the figures below give some idea of the extent of forgery, and the powers of experts to detect it. An American expert committee released its findings on some 2,000 stamps submitted to them as of doubtful authenticity. They certified 1,224 as genuine, found that 698 were not genuine and were unable to give a firm opinion in the case of seventy-eight.

The scientist in his perpetual quest for truth has produced the means of detecting most forgeries and, even now, more technical equipment is being experimented with. The quartz Lamp for instance, which produces mercury-vapour discharge and ultra-violet rays, has enabled experts, by studying the fluorescent effects caused by the rays, to detect minute differences in inks and paper, and traces of "ghost" postmarks. More recent experiment with X-rays has shown that a short wavelength some 10,000 times shorter than that of visible light, can give even better information than the ultra-violet rays. Recently Scotland Yard has set up a special Philatelic Department for the detection of forged and stolen philatelic material. Last year this department was responsible for sweeping a considerable number of rogues from the philatelic scene.

Appendix I

IDENTIFYING A STAMP

ALTHOUGH the name of the country of issue appears on the majority of postage stamps, beginners continually come up against the problem of identifying a stamp which does not bear the name of the country. Great Britain has never used its name on its stamps, which are identified by the monarch's head. As the collector gains experience he finds identification of country easier. Most stamps yield a clue, whether it be the currency, language, or design. The well-known chrysanthemum appears on the majority of Japanese stamps issued before 1947, the crescent with five-point star, or a crescent, identifies a Mohammedan country. With such clues it is not too difficult to flick through a catalogue and check the various places the stamp could have come from by studying the designs.

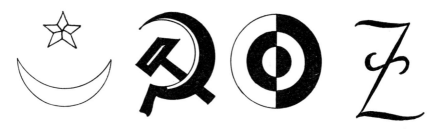

39. *Some of the emblems found on stamps that help in their identification.*
Crescent and star, Emblem of Turkey (This star-type from a local stamp);
Russia; Korea; Armenia

Many of the foreign-language names on stamps, like Belgique (Belgium), Danmark (Denmark), are readily understood. But there are quite a lot which are not easily identifiable. Hrvatska, for example, stands for Jugoslavia. And some alphabets are entirely different from the English alphabet. Here is a list which should help in identifying most stamps.

116

A and T	Annam and Tonquin
Açores	Azores
Afghanes	Afghanistan
Africa	Portuguese Africa
Afrique Equatoriale Française	French Equatorial Africa
Afrique Occidentale Française	French West Africa
Afrique Orientale Italiana	Italian East Africa
A.O.	Afrika Oost—Ruanda-Urundi
Algerie	Algeria
Amtlicher Verkehr	Wurttemberg
A Payer—Te Betalen	Belgium
A Percevoir (franc and centimes value)	Belgium
A Percevoir (paras or milliemes value)	Egypt
Argentina	Argentine
Avisporto	Denmark
B (on Straits Settlements)	Bangkok
Bani (on Austrian stamps)	Austrian occupation of Roumania
BATYM	Batum
Bayern	Bavaria
Bayer Post taxe	Bavaria
B.C.A.	British Central Africa
Belgien (on German stamps)	German occupation of Belgium
Belge or Belgique	Belgium
Bohmen und Mahren	Bohemia and Moravia (Czechoslovakia)
Bollo della Posta Napoletana	Naples
Bosnien-Herzegowina	Bosnia and Herzegovina
Brasil	Brazil
Braunschweig	Brunswick
Cabo Juby	Cape Juby
Cabo Verde	Cape Verde Island

C.C.C.P.	Russia
C.CH	Cochin China
Cechy a Morava	Bohemia and Moravia
C.E.F. (on India)	China Expeditionary Force
C.E.F. (on German colonies)	British occupation, Cameroons
Centesimi (on Austrian)	Austrian occupation of Italy
Centimes (on Austrian)	Austrian Post Offices in Crete
Ceskoslovensko	Czechoslovakia
Chiffre Taxe	France
Chine	French Post Offices in China
Colombia (with map of Panama)	Panama
Communicaciones	Spain
Confed. Granadina	Colombia (Granada Confederation)
Congo Belge	Belgian Congo
Continente	Portugal
Corée	Korea
Correio (value in reis)	Portugal, Brazil
Correos (with woman's head)	Spain, Cuba, Porto Rico, Philippine Is.
Correspondencia urgente	Spain
Cote d'Ivoire	Ivory Coast
Cote Francaise des Somalis	French Somali Coast
CPBNJA	Serbia
Danmark	Denmark
Dansk Vestindien	Danish West India
Deficit	Peru
Deutsche Reichspost	Germany
Deutsches Reich	Germany
Deutsch Neu-Guinea	German New Guinea
Deutsch Östafrika	German East Africa
Deutschösterreich	Austria
Deutsch Sudwestafrika	German South West Africa
Dienstmarke	Germany
Diligencia	Uruguay
D J	Djibouti
Drzava or Drzavna	Jugoslavia

E.E.F.	Palestine
Eesti	Estonia
E.F.O.	French Oceanic Establishments
Eire	Republic of Ireland
Elua Keneta	Hawaii
Emp Franc	France
Emp Ottoman	Turkey, Eastern Roumelia (Bulgaria)
Equateur	Ecuador
Escuelas	Venezuela
Espana, Espanola	Spain
Estados Unidos (or EE. UU) de Nueva Granada	Colombia

40. *1853 Imperf. Spain*

Estensi	Modena
Estero	Italian Levant Offices
Etablissements de l'Inde	French Indian Settlements
Etablissements de l'Oceanie	French Oceanic Settlements
Etat Ind du Congo	Belgian Congo
Ethiopie	Abyssinia

Falta de Porte	Bogus postage dues of Mexico
Filipinas	Philippine Islands
Franc (on Austrian)	Austrian P.O.s in Crete
Franco	Switzerland
Franco bollo	Italy, Roman States, Sardinia, Tuscany.
Franco Marke	Bremen
Franco Poste Bollo	Neapolitan Provinces and Italy
Franquicia postal	Spain
Freie Stadt Danzig	Danzig
Freimarke	Wurttemberg, Prussia
Frimaerke	Norway
Frimarke	Denmark
Furstentum Liechtenstein	Liechtenstein
G (on Cape of Good Hope stamps)	Griqualand West. Also used in Cape Colony
G and D (French Colonial)	Guadeloupe
G.E.A.	German East Africa (Tanganyika)
Georgie	Georgia
Gen-Gouv. Warschau	German occupation of Poland
Giuba	Jubaland
G.P.E.	Guadeloupe
Grand Liban	Lebanon
G.R.I.	New Guinea
Gross Deutsches Reich	Germany
Guiné	Portuguese Guinea
Guinée	French Guinea
Gultig 9 Armée	German occupation of Roumania
Guyane Française	French Guiana
Haute-Volta	Upper Volta
Helvetia	Switzerland
H.H. Nawab Shah Begam	Bhopal
Hrvatska	Jugoslavia
H.R.Z.G.L.	Holstein
I.E F. "D"	British Occupation, Mosul
Ile Rouad	Rouad Island

Imper. Reg.	Austrian P.O.s in Turkey
Impuesto de guerra	Spain, war tax.
Inde	French Indian Settlements
India Port	Portuguese India
Instruccion	Venezuela
Island	Iceland
Italia	Italy
Kaiser Konigl Österr	Austria
(Same with values in paras/piasters) (Same with values in centimes francs)	Austrian P.O.s in Turkey
	Austrian P.O.s in Crete
Kamerun	German Cameroons
Kärnten	Carinthia (Austria)
Karolinen	Caroline Is.
K.G.C.A. on Jugoslavia stamps	Carinthia (Austria)
Kgl. Post. Frm.	Denmark
(Same with value in cents)	Danish West Indies
K.K. Post. Stempel	Austria
(Same with values in centes)	Austrian Italy
Kongeligt Post Frimaerke	Denmark
K.P.H.T.H.	Crete
Kraljevina	Jugoslavia
Kraljevstvo	Jugoslavia
Kreuzer	Austria
K.u.K. Feldpost	Austrian military stamps
(Same with values in bani)	Austrian occupation of Roumania
K.u.K. Militarpost	Bosnia and Herzegovina
K. Wurtt. Post.	Wurttemberg
La Canea	Italian P.O.s in Crete
La Georgie	Georgia
Land-Post	Baden
Lattaquie	Latakia
Latvija	Latvia
Lei (on Austrian)	Austrian Occupation of Roumania
Libia	Libya
Lietuva	Lithuania

Lieutuvos	Lithuania
Litwa Srodkowa	Central Lithuania
L.Mc.L.	Trinidad
Losen	Sweden
Luxembourg	Luxemburg
Macau	Macao
Magyar	Hungary
Magyarorszag	Hungary
MAPKA	Russia
Marianen	Marianne Is.
Maroc	French P.O.s in Morocco. Also French protectorate from 1914. Now independent
Marruecos	Spanish Morocco
Marschall-Inseln	Marshall Is.
Mauritanie	Mauritania
Mejico	Mexico
Milit post Portomarke	Bosnia and Herzegovina
Moçambique	Mozambique
Modonesi	Modena
Montevideo	Uruguay
Moyen-Congo	Middle Congo
M.V. i. R.	German occupation of Roumania
Napoletana	Naples
N.C.E.	New Caledonia
Nederland	Holland
Ned Indie	Dutch Indies
Nederlandsch-Indie	Dutch Indies
N.F.	Nyasaland Field Force (Tanganyika)
Nieuwe Republiek	New Republic
Norddeutscher Postbezirk	North German Confederation
Norge	Norway
Nouvelle Caledonie	New Caledonia
Nouvelles Hebrides	New Hebrides
NOYTA	Russia

N.S.B.	Nossi Bé (Nòsy-bé)
N.S.W.	New South Wales
N.W. Pacific Islands	North West Pacific Islands, now New Guinea
N.Z.	New Zealand
Nyassa	Portuguese Nyassa
Oesterr, Oesterreich, Österreich	Austria
Oltre Giuba	Italian Jubaland
Orts Post	Switzerland
Ottoman, Ottomanes	Turkey
Pacchi Postale	Italy
Para	Egypt, Serbia, Turkey Levant
P.C.C.P.	Russia
Pesa (on German stamps)	German P.O.s in Turkey
P.G.S. (on Straits Settlements)	Perak Service stamps
Crescent, star and P in oval (on Strait Settlements)	Perak normal issues
Piaster (on German)	German P.O.s in Turkey
Pinsin	Ireland
ГOCCIΛ	Russia
Poczta Polska	Poland
Pohjois Inkeri	Ingermanland
Polska Poczta	Poland
Porte de Conduccion	Peru
Porte Franco	Peru
Porte de Mar	Mexico
Porteado	Portugal and colonies
Porto	Austria
Porto-Pflichtige Dienst-Sache	Wurttemberg
Posta Cesko-Slovenska	Czechoslovakia
Postage	Great Britain
Post Stamp	Hyderabad
Postas le n'ioc	Ireland
Postat e Qeverries	Albania
Poste Estensi	Modena
Poste Italiane	Italy

Poste Locale	Switzerland
Postes	Alsace and Lorraine, Belgium, Luxemburg
Postes de Coree	Korea
Postes Ethiopiennes	Abyssinia
Postes Ottomanes	Turkey
Postes Persanes	Persia
Poste Shquiptare	Albania
Poste Vaticane	Vatican City
Postgebiet Ob. Ost	German Eastern Army
Postzegel	Holland
Preussen	Prussia
Provincia de Macau	Macao
Provincie Modonesi	Modena
P.S.N.C. (Pacific Steam Navigation Co)	Peru
Qeverries	Albania
R	Jind
Rayon	Switzerland
Recargo	Spain
Regno d'Italia Venezia Giulia	Italy (Trieste)
Reichpost	Germany
R.F.	France and colonies
R.H.	Haiti (postage due)
Republica Dominicana	Dominican Republic
Republica Oriental	Uruguay
Repub Franc	France
Republique Georgienne	Georgia
Republique Libanaise	Lebanon
Rialtar Sealadac na heireann	Irish Provisional Government
R.O.	Eastern Roumelia
Romana, Romania, Romina	Roumania
Rumanien (on German)	German occupation of Roumania
Russisch-Polen (on German)	German occupation of Poland
Saargebiet	Saar District

Sache	Wurttemberg
Sachsen	Saxony
Saorstat eireann	Ireland
Segnatasse	Italy
Serbien	Austrian occupation of Serbia
S.H.	Schleswig-Holstein
S.H.S.	Jugoslavia
Shqipenia, Shqypnis, Shqyptare	Albania
Sld.	Austrian Italy
Slesvig	Schleswig
S.O.	Eastern Silesia
Soldi	Austrian Italy
Somalia Italiana	Italian Somaliland
S.P.M.	St. Pierre and Miquelon
S. Thomé e Principe	St. Thomas and Prince Is.
Sultanat d'Anjouan	Anjouan
Suomi	Finland
Suriname	Surinam
Sverige	Sweden
S.W.A.	South West Africa
Syrie, Syrienne	Syria
TAKCA	Bulgaria (postage due)
Te Betalen Port	Holland, Curacao, Dutch Indies, Surinam
T.E.O.	Cilicia, Syria
Tjenste post frimaerke	Danish West Indies
Toga	Tonga
Toscano	Tuscany
Tunisie	Tunis
U.A.R.	United Arab Republic (Egypt)
U.G.	Uganda
Uku Leta	Hawaii
Ultramar	Cuba, Porto Rico
U.S.	United States
Van Diemen's Land	Tasmania

Venezia Giulia (on Italy)	Italy (Trieste)
Venezia Tridentina (on Italy)	Italy (Trentino)
Vom empfanger einzuziehen	Danzig
Wurtt.	Wurttemberg
Y.C.C.P.	Ukraine
YKPAIHCЬKA	Ukraine
Ykp H.P.	West Ukraine
Z. Afr. Republiek	S. African Republic (Transvaal)
Z.A.R.	Transvaal
Zeitungs	Austria, Austrian Italy
Zuid West Africa	South West Africa.

There are some stamps which do not use our alphabet or which do not have any letters upon them which give a clue to their identification. But the best way to get to know them is to study the stamp catalogues.

Appendix II

PHILATELIC TERMS

ADHESIVE. A stamp originally issued with gum on the back so that it can be stuck down. The first adhesive stamp was the Penny Black of Great Britain, 1840.

AERO PHILATELY. Anything to do with air-mail stamps and flown covers, including balloon and pigeon mail.

AIR MAIL STAMPS. Stamps produced for use on air-mail letters.

ALBINO. Any part of a stamp design impressed (by error) where no ink is used—most common on embossed stamps.

ANILINE. A chemical used to produce brilliant colouring. It can usually be detected because aniline shows through the back of a stamp. Aniline is derived from coal-tar.

ALPHABET LETTERS. Various type alphabets are recognized. They are used in the early line-engraved issues of Great Britain and are of major importance in identification.

A.P.O. Army Post Office.

ARROW BLOCK. A block of stamps with sheet margin attached showing an arrow indicating to counter clerks a specific division (usually half) of a complete sheet.

BACK STAMPED. Said of an envelope or folded letter, with a date-stamp on the reverse, indicating the route a letter has travelled or the date of its arrival in the town, or country, of destination.

BALLON MONTÉ. Used to denote that the mail was carried in a manned balloon. Balloon non-monté—in an unmanned balloon.

BALLOON POST. Delivery by balloon.

BALTICUM. Sometimes used to denote the Baltic States.

BANTAMS. War issues of South Africa made in miniature to save paper (1939-45).

BARRED. Heavy bar cancellation.

BATONNÉ PAPER. Paper watermarked with spaced lines.

BILINGUAL PAIRS. Many South African stamps are printed in pairs alternating with English and Afrikaans.

BISECTS. Stamps which have been cut in half (usually diagonally) i.e. an 8d. stamp cut and used as a 4d. on the envelope. Such stamps have been permitted by many countries during emergencies.

41. *A bisected Elizabeth II 8d. of Great Britain—unofficially allowed by many Post Offices when, at the increase of postage rates, 4d. stamps ran short*

BISHOP MARK. Famous circular handstamp mark introduced in 1661 by Henry Bishop who said of it, "A stamp is invented".

BLEUTÉ PAPER. Paper that is blued by the manufacturing process.

BLIND PERFORATION. Where the perforator has only dented the paper.

BLOCK. A group of stamps still joined together; of four stamps or more and not in strip form.

BOGUS. A stamp not issued by any recognized authority. Stamps have appeared of fictitious countries. Also used when an unauthorized overprint is used on a genuine stamp.

BOOKLET. Little books of stamps issued at post-offices.

BULL'S EYES. Nick-name for the first issues of Brazil because of their oval-shaped design.

BURELÉ. A wavy line or dotted pattern of fine network.

BUREAU PRINT. Stamps pre-cancelled at the United States Bureau of Printing.

42. *Brazil bull's eyes. This particular strip fetched £11,500 at a Stanley Gibbon's Auction in 1969*

CACHET. A mark on mail showing a special occurrence, like a first day cover, expedition or special air-flight.

CANCELLATION. The all embracing term for marks on a stamp to prevent its re-use. These can be postmarks, pen-marks, words like "Specimen", hole-punches and so on.

CANCELLED BY COMPLAISANCE. Where the postmark has been carefully put on to oblige a collector.

CANCELLED-TO-ORDER. Stamps specially cancelled, usually in considerable quantity, and sold to dealers without being used on mail.

CANTONAL STAMPS. Stamps issued by Cantonal administrations before the Swiss Confederation issues.

CARLIST STAMPS. Stamps issued by Don Carlos in 1873–74 in Spain.

CARRIER'S STAMPS. Specially produced stamps to pay the carriers to or from a post-office, in the days when there was no organization to deliver house-to-house. Normally applied to certain U.S. stamps

CENTRED. Used where a stamp design is balanced equally from the four margins. Off-centre stamps are usually worth less.

COIL STAMPS. Stamps produced for sale in machines—usually outside post-offices. They are reeled in a single-line and often they have a sideways watermark. They are also known as rolls.

COLLEGE STAMPS. Oxford and Cambridge colleges used special stamps for their messenger services in 1871–86. The Postmaster-General stopped the practice since it infringed his monopoly.

COLOUR TRIALS. Proofs made to show how a stamp would look in different colours.

COLUMN. The vertical lines in a sheet of stamps.

COMBINATION COVER. Where stamps of more than one country are found on a cover.

COMPOUND PERFORATION. Where the gauge of the perforations on a stamp is not the same on all four sides.

CONTROL LETTERS. Letters or numbers formerly used in sheet margins of British stamps so that officials can tell to which printing order the stamps relate.

COVER. The envelope or wrapper to which a stamp is attached. If not complete the stamp is described as "on piece".

CUT-SQUARE. Stamps that have been impressed on envelopes, postcards, etc., are described "cut-square" when carefully cut out and squared off.

CYLINDER NUMBERS. British sheets printed by rotary photogravure from cylindrical plates have figures in the margins showing the number of the cylinder.

DEFACED PLATE. Printing plates deliberately scratched to stop them being used again after official withdrawal of the stamp printed by that plate.

DEFINITIVE ISSUES. The normal issues of a country as against commemoratives, charities etc.

DICKINSON PAPER. Paper with continuous silk threads in it. This paper was used for Mulready envelopes.

DIE. The actual engraved piece of metal which is sometimes called the original master-die. It is normally used for the purpose of reproducing replica impressions on a "plate" by which the stamps are printed.

DIE PROOF. A trial print of a stamp design from a die. Usually produced in black.

DOMINICAL LABELS. Labels attached to Belgian stamps between 1893–1914 stating that the letter is not to be delivered on a Sunday.

DUTY PLATE. Used to print the value on a stamp. Thus every stamp in a set requires a separate duty plate. The general design applying to the set is printed from the key plate.

ENGINE TURNED. The intricate design used for background and worked by a Rose-engine.

ENGRAVED. In the stamp world this means a stamp printed from plates engraved in recess. More correctly described as line-engraved.

ENTIRE. A complete envelope, postcard or wrapper with stamps attached. Often used as an alternative word to cover, but implies stamps attached, as against pre-adhesive covers.

ERROR. Where there is something wrong with the stamp compared to the normal issue—and meaning that the stamp has been issued by the Post Office, as against printers' waste etc.

ESSAYS. Stamp designs submitted for an issue but not accepted.

EXPERT COMMITTEES. Certain organizations, notably the Royal Philatelic Society, London, and the British Philatelic Association issue certificates with photographs attached, of stamps on which they give an opinion of genuineness for a fee.

FACE VALUE. The denomination of the actual stamp and the price paid for it at a Post Office during its postal use.

FACSIMILE. A copy of a stamp which is exactly the same as the original except for some marking denoting that it is not genuine.

FAKE. A stamp that has been altered in some way in order to deceive a collector.

FARMERS' PARCEL STAMPS. Uruguay issued these in 1929; triangulars, they were specially produced for farmers' parcels.

FIRST DAY COVER. Envelope bearing stamp used and postmarked on its first day of use.

FISCAL. A stamp used for other purposes than the post.

43. *A "dummy" first day cover prepared by the G.P.O. to publicize the Shakespeare commemorative stamps.*

FLAW. An imperfection in the design of a printed stamp occasioned by a defect in the printing plate or cylinder. The flaw appears constantly on all stamps from that plate in the same position on the sheet and assists collectors "plating" the stamps.

FRANKS. Free postage. At one time Members of Parliament were able to send letters free-of-charge. Special marks were used to show that the letters were free of postage. Sometimes they were simply the signature of the sender. Modern "franks" refer to letters from soldiers on active service and government correspondence sent free.

FRONT. The obverse of an envelope.

GENERAL COLLECTOR. A non-specialist collector.

GRANITE PAPER. Paper containing small fibres clearly visible on the reverse of the stamp.

GRILL. Minute dots, patterned and embossed on many early U.S.A. stamps. The grill breaks the paper surface and allows postmark to penetrate and thus prevents the cancellation of a stamp being removed so that it could be used again.

GUARANTEE. Some stamp dealers put a small mark on the reverse of a stamp to show that it is genuine and guaranteed by them. Some collectors do not agree with this practice as it is a mark on the stamp not made by the Post Office and can be forged the same way as a stamp.

GUIDE LINES. Barely visible lines used as marks by the printers laying down the impressions on a plate. When the guide marks have not been wiped off properly traces of them show.

GUM. The sticky substance on the reverse of a mint stamp. Some rarities are re-gummed to deceive collectors.

GUTTERS. The area between stamps for perforation.

HAIR LINES. Marks used on some English stamps to show the authorities which plate impression the stamp came from.

HAND-STAMP. A postal marking struck by hand as opposed to a machine cancellation.

HAND-STRUCK. Describes a stamp impression struck by hand from a die, rather than being printed from a plate in a machine.

HARROW PERFORATION. A form of perforating used extensively by some mid-European countries (Hungary, Austria) in which the entire sheet is perforated at one strike.

HINGE. A stamp mount.

IMPERFORATE. A stamp that is not perforated and needs cutting from the sheet.

IMPRIMATUR SHEET. The sheet of stamps registered at Somerset House. A practice that has died out. Stamps from such sheets have come on the market. They are normally imperforate even when the issued stamps are perforate.

IMPRINT. The printer's name or mark.

INTAGLIO. Engraving in recess.

INVALIDATED. Stamps officially declared no longer valid for postage are said to be invalidated or demonetized

44. *Grill; used particularly on early United States stamps so that postmark ink would seep through and thus prevent the re-use of the stamp*

INVERTED. Upside-down. Often part of a design will be inverted, such as the head of a monarch or the figure of the denomination.

IVORY HEAD. English 1d. and 2d. stamps of 1841 are found with the Queen's head in white on the reverse caused through some chemical reaction which causes blueing of the paper. These stamps are called ivory heads.

JUBILEE LINE. The coloured line put round the sheets of stamps as a protection against the edges of the plates becoming worn. It was first used in the Jubilee Year of Queen Victoria.

KILLER. A term used to describe particularly heavy obliterations.

KNIFE. The unfolded sheet of paper used to make an envelope.

LOCALS. Stamps made to serve a particular area only. Usually issued by private companies or municipalities.

MARGINAL MARKINGS. Sheets of stamps have various markings in the margins which have an important significance to collectors as they simplify the matter of plating stamps. Such markings include control numbers, cylinder numbers, plate serials, the names of the printers, arrow marks showing the equal divisions of the sheet and values showing the total value of the sheet. In addition, decorative lines appear for the sole purpose of preventing forgers from using the stamp paper to reproduce stamps. United States stamps have electric eye markings and British stamps have colour registry marks. Sometimes a hole will be found for perforation registry. A popular form

45. *Attractive marginal markings. Israel Chess Olympics*

134

of marginal mark collecting is that of the imprint blocks. These contain the name of the printer.

MATRIX. The impression taken from the original die which is used to make exact copies.

MINIATURE SHEET. Specially produced sheets of stamps sometimes containing only one stamp; usually for commemorative purposes.

MINT. A stamp in its original perfect state complete with gum.

MUESTRA. The Spanish for "specimen" found on many Latin American stamps.

MULREADY. The first envelope issued in 1840 and designed by William Mulready, R.A., used in Great Britain and pre-paid. They are known as Mulreadys.

NEW ISSUE SERVICE. The service set up by many dealers to provide collectors with the new issues of countries as they are issued.

OBLITERATION. A general term to describe a postal cancellation. It can refer to one that does not give the date or time.

OFFICIAL IMITATIONS. Government-authorized reproductions of stamps after the original dies were no longer available—as against a reprint from the original dies.

ON PIECE. Where a stamp is on part of an envelope or wrapper.

OVERPRINT. Marks placed on a stamp after its original printing. Many collectors use the term to denote markings that do not alter the face value and thus distinguish it from the word "surcharge".

PACKET BOAT. A boat that carried mail under contract to the G.P.O.

PANE. A block of stamps with four gutter margins forming part only of a complete sheet.

PAQUEBOT. Used to describe cancellations applied to mail posted on board ship and handed in at the next port of call. The word "paquebot" in a cancellation thus accounts for, say, French stamps bearing a South African cancellation, as when a French ship calls at Capetown or Durban.

PATRIOTIC COVER. During the American Civil War many different propaganda designs were put on envelopes by both the Union and the Confederacy.

PERFORATION. Where the edges of a stamp have been punched by a machine to take away portions of the paper. This produces small circular holes between stamps and enables them to be parted easily. Where a stamp has been rouletted instead of perforated it means that the paper has not actually been taken away; only cut. The gauge of a perforation is measured by the number of holes in a space of 2 cms. Hence, Perf 12½, Perf 15, denote the number of holes in that space.

PHILATELIC BUREAUX. Officially-appointed bureaux set up by various governments and attached to the post offices to deal with stamp collectors.

PHILATELIC CONGRESS OF GREAT BRITAIN. An organization started in 1909 to which philatelic societies from all over the Commonwealth are affiliated. They discuss matters relating to the hobby.

PHILATELIST. Someone who studies postage stamps. From the Greek *philos* (loving) and *ateleia* (exemption from tax).

PHOSPHOR. All current G.B. stamps are phosphor. If the stamp is held so that light reflects from the printed surface the band or bands of phosphor will be seen as a dulled area on the stamp. Phosphor is used to facilitate electronic sorting machines which face letters the correct way ready for cancellation. Introduced first in 1959 certain areas were used "experimentally" and these stamps can therefore be collected phosphor and non-phosphor. Phosphor replaced the Graphite Line which consisted of vertical lines of graphite in black on the backs of stamps in 1957 when experiments were first carried out with electronic sorting machines.

PLATE. A "plate" is the actual sheet of metal or other material from which the stamps are printed. It often happens that more than one plate is used and that slight differences between the plates are noticeable. Stamps from such plates are described, Plate I, Plate II, etc.

PLATE NUMBERS. Stamps produced by Great Britain and the Empire have numbers in the margins denoting the order of the plates. Some stamps, including all those issued by Great Britain between 1858 and 1880 have plate numbers on the actual stamps as well.

POSTAGE DUE. Special stamps, not really postage stamps, used to make up the deficiency when a letter or postal packet has been insufficiently paid. The charge is payable by the addressee.

POSTAL HISTORY. Matters appertaining to the postal systems of the world from the very beginning of the interchange of messages. A student of postal history is not necessarily a stamp collector.

POSTAL STATIONERY. Envelopes, postcards and wrappers which have stamps printed on them.

PRE-STAMP COVERS. Covers sent through the post before the adhesive stamp was invented. Many of these have markings of great interest, such as "Penny Post" "2d. paid" etc.

PRINTER'S WASTE. Stamp material thrown away by the printers because of defects. Sometimes items of this sort come on the market. They are not genuine errors.

PRISONER OF WAR POSTS. Through agreement with the Universal Postal Union and the International Red Cross all letters of prisoners of war interned in neutral or belligerent nations are sent free, except for special charges such as air mail.

PROOFS. Printings taken for a proposed issue to show the authorities what they will look like. These can be sub-divided into engraver's proofs, made to show the progress of the stamp; die-proofs to show that the die is ready for making a plate; plate-proofs, the final proof taken from the plate to show that it is ready for actual stamp printing. Also there are colour-proofs from which the authorities choose the actual colours of a stamp.

PROVISIONALS. Stamps used during a shortage of normal issues for a limited period. Normally they are ordinary stamps overprinted or surcharged.

PUNCH-PERFORATED STAMPS. Sooner or later the collector will come across stamps which have perforated holes punched into the design of the stamp. Many collectors regard these as "damaged" and, therefore, such stamps are very much cheaper than those without such punch holes. But it would be wrong to dismiss them altogether and, in fact, there are specialized collections of this type of stamp known to collectors as "perfins". At one time Stanley Gibbons catalogued certain punch-perforated stamps but later catalogues have dropped them—another reason for their cheapness, since the majority of collectors other than specialists regard the catalogues as the "bible" of the stamp world.

But Sudan stamps officially perforated with the letters "S.G." for Sudan Government and "A.S." for Army Service, cannot be ignored by the specialist of Sudan. Consequently they fetch good prices.

The vast majority of such perforated stamps are the issues of private firms, and the object of the perforated initials or marks is simply to prevent theft. These do not hold the same value as stamps of the same issue unperforated, but they are collectable and a great many firms can be traced through the initials punched into the stamps.

Other punch perforations can be found on many foreign stamps, denoting various things. Some Hungarian stamps have three "pinhole" punch marks in the shape of a triangle, centrally placed through the stamps. Uruguay issued stamps with two stars perforated through them to denote official air stamps. Spain used a single, but quite large, punch hole to denote telegraphic (as distinct from postal) use.

QUADRILLÉ. Paper watermarked or printed with crossed lines which causes a pattern of small squares.

QUARTZ LAMP. An invention which enables philatelists to examine stamps under ultra-violet ray. It shows degrees of fluorescence which indicate whether a stamp has been repaired or tampered with in any way such as having markings erased. It is of importance in detecting reprints where different inks have been used.

RECONSTRUCTION. Another word for plating. Many collectors "reconstruct" a sheet of stamps using pairs, strips and blocks put into the sheet position (with the aid of minute flaws which can be studied and recognized) they occupied when first printed by the plate.

RE-ENTRY. Official repair to a worn or damaged design on a plate, after stamps have been printed from that plate.

REMAINDERS. When stamps are withdrawn from issue there are often stocks of them left which are referred to as remainders. Some countries sell these off cheaply to dealers which unbalances the previous collectors' value of that stamp.

REPRINTS. Impressions taken from original plates after the original printings have stopped. Because they are made from the original plates reprints can be extremely difficult to detect. The main differences are gum, paper, watermark or colour. On occasion reprints have been allowed for postage. Although many rare stamps have quite common reprint counterparts, it also happens that reprints can be worth substantially more than originals!

RETOUCH. When metal has been added to, or removed from, a faulty part of a plate a retouch is made to the printing surface.

ROULETTE. As distinct from perforation, rouletting is a form of separating stamps by making cuts on the paper without removing any paper. Perforation, on the other hand, removes small circles of paper.

ST. ANDREW'S CROSS. Some early Austrian issues of stamps did not take up a complete sheet. The blank spaces were printed with a cross to stop the paper being used by forgers. They also occur in some early booklets of British stamps (King Edward VII) which sold for 2s., but only had stamps valued at 1s. 11½d., the St. Andrew's Cross filling the space of the missing ½d. stamp.

SEEBECKS. Nicholas F. Seebeck made a deal with the governments of Ecuador, Honduras, Nicaragua and Salvador to supply them with a new issue of stamps every year, free of charge, on condition that at the end of each year he could have the remainders and the original plates. With these he was able to sell to collectors at greatly reduced rates and print more stamps as needed.

SE-TENANT. A term used to describe two stamps of different design or colour that are joined together.

SET. The full range of an issue of stamps, e.g. Great Britain current set from ½d. to £1.

SHIP LETTERS. Letters carried by ships without a Post Office contract. Special postmarks were used to denote this, such as "SHIP LETTER" and "S". The captain of the ship collected a fee for carrying the letters and this was charged to the addressees on delivery.

SPECIMEN. A stamp marked to show that it is a specimen for record purposes only. Often the word "Specimen" will be perforated or printed on to the stamp, showing that it has no postal value.

SPECULATIVE ISSUES. Issues by countries for no other reason than to attract collectors to buy them.

STAMP CURRENCY. During shortages of coin, authority has sometimes been given for mint postage stamps to serve as coin. This occurred notably in the United States during the Civil War where special cases were made to hold such stamps.

TÊTE-BÊCHE. A term describing two stamps joined together where one is upside down.

THEMATICS. Used to describe subject collecting, e.g. art on stamps, flowers on stamps.

TIED. Where the postmark is partly on the stamp and partly on the cover the stamp is referred to as "tied" to the cover with such and such a postmark.

T.P.O. Travelling Post Office.

UNIVERSAL POSTAL UNION. All countries with an organized postal system belong to the Union, which was founded in 1874, and international relations in postal services and charges are administered by the Union.

UNUSED. A stamp which has not been postmarked but does not necessarily have gum on the back—as distinct from mint.

USED. A stamp which has been postmarked in some way.

VARIETY. A stamp which differs from the normal through some defect in the printing or plate.

VIGNETTE. The central portrait on a stamp or main design.

WATERMARK. A marking produced in the paper during the process of manufacture.

WRECK COVER. Mail salvaged from wrecked ships.

46. *Famous Hungarian bridges. Most of the world's well known bridges are depicted on stamps and can form an interesting thematic collection*

Appendix III

LIST OF FURTHER READING

THERE are many books dealing with the hobby of philately. This list does not pretend to be complete but merely to give a range of books which covers all the important aspects of the hobby.

ARMSTRONG D. and HARRISON M. *New Approach to Stamp Collecting.*

EASTON, J., *Postage Stamps in the Making.*

GIBBONS, S., *Great Britain Specialized Stamp Catalogue* Vol I: *Queen Victoria*, Vol II: *Edward VII to George VI.*

LOWE, ROBSON, *The British Postage Stamp*

MACKAY, J. A., *World of Stamps; Money in Stamps; Invest in Stamps*

NARBETH, C., *Investing in Stamps; The Stamps of Great Britain, A Beginners' Guide*

PHILLIPS, S. and RANG, *How to Arrange and Write up a Stamp Collection*

POOLE, B. W. H., *The Pioneer Stamps of the British Empire*

Royal Philatelic Society, *The Postage Stamps of Great Britain* (various parts)

STAFF, F., *The Penny Post 1680–1918*; *The Transatlantic Mail*

WATSON, J., *Stamps and Music; Stamps and Railways*

The most widely used catalogues in Great Britain are:

BRIDGER AND KAY: *Commonwealth Catalogue King George VI*

GIBBONS: *Simplified Stamp Catalogue (The World)*
        Part I British Commonwealth
        Part II Europe and Colonies
        Part III America, Asia and Africa
        Elizabethan Postage Stamp Catalogue

JOHN LISTER: *Queen Elizabeth II Catalogue*

URCH HARRIS AND Co. LTD: *Catalogue of Queen Elizabeth II Stamps*

WOODSTOCK: *Catalogue of British Elizabethan Stamps*

MAGAZINES

Suggested magazines to read:

Weekly: *Stamp Collecting*
             Editor: Kenneth F. Chapman
             42 Maiden Lane, London, W.C.2.

Bi-weekly: *Philatelic Magazine*
Editor: O. Newport
16 John Adam Street, London, W.C.2.

Monthly: *The Stamp Magazine*
Editor: Arthur Blair
Link House, Dingwall Avenue, Croydon, Surrey, CR9 2TA.

Gibbons Stamp Monthly
Editor: Russell Bennett
Drury House, Russell Street, London, W.C.2.

Appendix IV

LIST OF USEFUL ADDRESSES

The British Philatelic Association
446 Strand, London, W.C.2

Founded in 1926 this is one of the most important philatelic organizations. They publish yearly the Philatelic Societies Year Book which lists all societies, etc., affiliated to the B.P.A., details about them and their yearly programmes. Every two months the B.P.A. publishes a magazine *Philately* and also runs a valuable service to collectors through its Expert Committee which issues certificates concerning the genuineness of stamps submitted. Although these are only given as "opinions" they carry great weight in the philatelic world. Members get special rates for use of the Expert Committee and, for members only, there is a Collectors' Advisory Bureau which, at very little cost, identifies by code medium class stamps, e.g. F—forgery, FO—forged overprint etc. The code "E" indicates that the stamp is recommended for submission to the Expert Committee for further opinion and certificate. Full details of the B.P.A. are sent out from their headquarters on request.

The Royal Philatelic Society, London.
Secretary: G. South, 41 Devonshire Place, London, W.1
Like the B.P.A. this is a very important organization which offers special services to its members. The patron is Her Majesty Queen Elizabeth II.
National Philatelic Society.
Secretary: G. H. Simpson, 44 Fleet Street, London, E.C.4
A large society with a good library at the Fleet Street headquarters and an important exchange packet circuit.
Philatelic Congress of Great Britain
Secretary: E. F. Hugen, 3 The Woodlands, London Road, Withdean, Brighton 6, Sussex
Founded in 1909, the Congress meets annually in various parts of the country. In 1949 Congress instituted the Melville Memorial Junior Prizes. These are annual awards to juniors of four age groups. Rules and details are available from the Secretary as above.
The Scottish Philatelic Congress
Secretary: A. McEwan, 8 Forbes Street, Alloa, Clackmannanshire

County Federations
East Midlands Federation of Stamps Clubs
Secretary: G. A. Powell, 181 Mayors Walk, Peterborough, Northants
Federation of Employee-Membership Philatelic Societies
Secretary: J. F. Dawes, 1 Locarno Road, Greenford, Middlesex
Association of Essex Philatelic Societies
Secretary: D. Venman, 17 Hilary Crescent, Rayleigh, Essex
Kent Federation of Philatelic Societies
Secretary: V. A. Daniels, 22 Hunters Way, Gillingham, Kent
Federation of Middlesex and Associated Philatelic Societies
Secretary: Mrs. K. Goodman, 110 Brunswick Road, London, W.5
Midland Philatelic Federation
Secretary: J. L. Adams, 15 Smirrells Road, Hall Green, Birmingham 28, Warwickshire

North of England Philatelic Association
Secretary: G. J. Riddle, 18 Varo Terrace, Stockton-on-Tees, Co. Durham
North-Western Federation of Philatelic Societies
Secretary: G. Barber, B.Sc., A.R.T.C.S., 172 Brooklands Road, Sale, Cheshire
Federation of Surrey Philatelic Societies
Secretary: D. W. Boydell, E.R.D., Rutland, 27 Nonsuch Walk, Cheam, Sutton, Surrey.
Association of Sussex Philatelic Societies
Secretary: Miss A. Whitehead, 7 Somerhill Court, Holland Road, Hove, Sussex
Wessex Philatelic Association
Secretary: F. G. A. Dolbear, 26 Fairpark Road, Exeter, Devon
Wiltshire Philatelic Federation
Secretary: L. C. H. Morgan, 22 Southbroom Place, Devizes, Wiltshire
Yorkshire Philatelic Association
Secretary: H. Clarkson, 70 Foundry Walk, Leeds 8

There are two national societies concerned with the general study of postal history. They are:

Postal History Society
Secretary: F. Walker, June Cottage, North Street, Petworth, Sussex
Society of Postal Historians
Secretary: V. Denis Vandervelde, 25 Sinclair Grove, London, N.W.11

Town and City Clubs
There are a great number of local clubs. The majority of these are listed in the B.P.A. Year Book.

Specialist Societies
Aero
Secretary: R. D. B. Scott, 103 Stamford Court, London, W.6.
American Stamp Club of Great Britain
Secretary: Mrs. S. Nicholson, 18 Pinfold Road, Solihull, Warwickshire
Anglo-Boer War
Secretary: J. H. Rathbone, "Allways", Rudheath, Northwich, Cheshire

Association of Austrian Philatelists
Secretary: Tom Marsh, 14 Sopwell Lane, St. Albans, Herts
Australian Commonwealth Specialists' Society of Great Britain
Secretary: Prof. V. W. Dix, 8 Shandon Close, Tunbridge Wells, Kent
Austrian Stamp Club of Great Britain
Secretary: J. W. Syddall, 21 Moscow Road, Edgeley Park, Stockport, Cheshire
Belgian Study Circle
Secretary: Dr. C. E. Gallagher, Killiecrankie, 196 Main Road, Sidcup, Kent
British Air Mail Society
Secretary: Mrs. C. M. Gray, 35 Southwood Road, New Eltham, London, S.E.9
British Air Mail (Northern Group)
Secretary: W. Colling White, "Westholme", Westerton Road, Leeholme, Bishop Auckland, Co. Durham
British Association of Palestine-Israel Philately
Secretary: M. Seshold, 39 Lullington Garth, Woodside Park, London, N.12
British Postmark Society
Secretary: G. R. Pearson, 42 Corrance Road, London, S.W.2
British Society of Russian Philately
Secretary: 7. Lloyd, The Retreat, Queens Road, West Bergholt, Colchester, Essex
British West Africa Study Circle
Secretary: H. B. Macmillan, Rowditch Printing Works, Derby
British West Indies Study Circle
Secretary: P. T. Saunders, Little Caymans, Kingsthorne, Hereford
Canadian Philatelic Society of Great Britain
Secretary: Dr. C. W. Hollingsworth, 17 Mellish Road, Walsall, Staffs
Channel Islands Specialists Society
Secretary: O. W. Newport, Farm Cottage, 33 Halfway Street, Sidcup, Kent
China Philatelic Society of London
Secretary: E. N. Lane, Kingsland, Westwell, Ashford, Kent.
East Anglia Postal History Study Circle
Secretary: G. M. Stephenson, 47 King Street, Royston, Herts.
Egypt Study Circle
Secretary: E. H. Proctor, 22 Chancellor House, Mount Ephraim, Tunbridge Wells, Kent

Essex Postal History
  Secretary: E. W. Goss, 9 Connaught Avenue, Grays, Essex
Fine Arts
  Secretary: F. W. Panter, 10 Pulteney Street, Bath, Somerset
The Forces Postal History Society
  Secretary: W. Garrard, 7 Hillbeck Way, Greenford, Middlesex
France and Colonies Philatelic Society
  Secretary: C. L. Easton, 58 Park Avenue, Sittingbourne, Kent
Germany and Colonies Philatelic Society
  Secretary: O. Winter, 24 Tennyson Road, London, N.W.7
Glasgow Thematic
  Secretary: Miss M. G. Wilson, 30 Viewfield, Airdrie, Lanarkshire
Great Britain Philatelic Society
  Secretary: P. J. D'arcy, 67 Cissbury Ring South, London, N.12
Great Britain Study Circle
  Secretary: James W. Brewer, "Downview", The Ridgewaye, Southborough, Tunbridge Wells, Kent.
Guild of St. Gabriel (G.B. and Ireland)
  Secretary: Miss Kathleen Morgan, 36 St. George's Road, St. Margaret's, Twickenham, Middlesex
Helvetia Philatelic Society
  Secretary: Mrs. E. J. Rawnsley, 32 Ethelbert Gardens, Gants Hill, Ilford, Essex
Hong Kong Study Circle
  Secretary: W. R. Wellsted, Langite Works, South Chingford, London, E.4
India Study Circle
  Secretary: B. T. Cheverton, 42 Ashcroft Road, Luton, Bedfordshire
Irish Philatelic Circle
  Secretary: T. Stewart Telfer, 1 Briarview Court, Handsworth, Avenue, Highams Park, London, E.4
Japanese Stamp Group
  Secretary: A. D. Taylor Smith, Clare Cottage, Rowledge, Farnham, Surrey
King George The Sixth Collectors' Society
  Secretary: F. R. Saunders, 65 Westbrooke Avenue, West Hartlepool, Co. Durham
Liechtenstein Study Circle
  Secretary: J. Beken, 30 Lingwood Gardens, Isleworth, Middlesex
Lundy Island Specialists Society
  Secretary: B. N. D. Chinchen, 97 Chamberlayne Road, Eastleigh, Hants

Magyar Philatelic Society of G.B.
   Secretary: E. Homolya, 406 Didsbury Road, Heaton Mersey, Stockport, Cheshire
Malta Study Circle
   Secretary: R. F. Whitehead, 55 Ridham Avenue, Kemsley, Sittingbourne, Kent
Malaya Study Group (U.K. Branch)
   Secretary: G. P. T. Peters, 14 Beechdale Road, London, S.W.2
Meter Stamp Study Group
   Secretary: J. C. Mann, 19 Chartham Road, London, S.E.25
Netherlands Philatelic Circle
   Secretary: F. Waine, 11 Acre Rise, The Grove, Baildon, Shipley, Yorks.
New Zealand Society of Great Britain
   Secretary: Noel Turner, Gladstone House, High Road, Wood Green, London, N.22
Orange Free State Study Circle
   Secretary: W. B. Marriott, 46 Kingswood Gardens, Leeds 8
Oriental Philatelic Association of London
   Secretary: A. D. Taylor Smith, Clare Cottage, Rowledge, Farnham, Surrey
Pacific Islands Study Circle of Great Britain
   Secretary: A. F. Young, 58 Livesay Crescent, Worthing, Sussex
Papuan-New Guinea Philatelic Society
   Secretary: W. G. Colbran, 64 Sussex Road, Haywards Heath, Sussex
Persian Study Circle
   Secretary: Mrs. J. Cohen, 11 Llwyn-y-Grant Road, Penylan, Cardiff, South Wales
Polar Postal History Society of Great Britain
   Secretary: H. E. J. Evans, Court House, Court Lane, Cosham, Portsmouth, Hants.
Polish Philatelic Society
   Secretary: T. L. Krynski, 18 Ross Road, Wallington, Surrey
Portuguese Study Group
   Secretary: L. Thompson, 103ª Rugby Avenue, Wembley, Middlesex
Postal History Society
   Hon. Secretary: Frederick Walker, June Cottage, North Street, Petworth, Sussex

Precancel Stamp Society
Secretary: C. C. D. Seggins, The Cottage, Ongar Road, Abridge, Romford, Essex

Psywar
Secretary: Peter H. Robbs, 8 Ridgway Road, Barton Seagrave, Kettering, Northants.

Railway Philatelic Group
Secretary: R. A. Kirk, 59a Hartley Road, Kirkby-in-Ashfield, Nottingham

Rhodesian Study Circle
Secretary: F. C. Donaldson, 14 Makepeace Avenue, Highgate, London, N.6

Sarawak Specialists'
Secretary: Dr. D. A. Pocock, Ravelston, South View Road, Pinner, Middlesex

The Scandinavia Collectors' Society
Secretary: H. T. Pritchett, 3 Mark's Avenue, Ongar, Essex

Scottish Postmark Group
Secretary: D. C. Jefferies, 11 Craigcrook Avenue, Edinburgh 4

Scout Stamps Collectors Club
Secretary: H. L. Fears, Rose Cottage, Selmeston, Polegate, Surrey

Security Endorsement and Perfin Society of Great Britain
Secretary: R. Bowman, "Gwel Marten", Beechfield, Frilsham, Newbury, Berks

South African Collectors' Society
Secretary: W. A. Page, 138 Chastilian Road, Dartford, Kent

Spanish Civil War Study Group
Secretary: R. G. Shelley, 31 Guildford Street, Brighton, Sussex

Spanish Philatelic Society
Secretary: R. G. Shelley, 31 Guildford Street, Brighton, Sussex

Thailand Philatelic Society
Secretary: P. E. Collins, 85 St. John's Road, Woking, Surrey

T.P.O. and Seapost Society
Secretary: C. Kidd, 9 Beech Avenue, Northenden, Manchester 22

Transvaal Study Circle
Secretary: Major H. M. Criddle, 23 Longcroft Avenue, Banstead, Surrey

Appendix V

AUCTIONS

SOME of the more important auction rooms are listed below. Collectors wishing to know more about auctions should write to the addresses.

CAVENDISH AUCTIONS,
    4 Curzon Street, Derby
CITY OF LONDON PHILATELIC AUCTIONS,
    170 Bishopsgate, London, E.C.2
H. R. HARMER LTD., INTERNATIONAL STAMP AUCTIONEERS,
    41 New Bond Street, London, W.1
STANLEY GIBBONS AUCTIONS LTD.,
    (Formerly Harmer, Rooke and Co. Ltd.) Drury House, Russell Street, Covent Garden, London, W.C.2
LONDON AND BRIGHTON STAMP AUCTIONS,
    98 Queens Road, Brighton
LONDON STAMP EXCHANGE,
    5 Buckingham Street, Strand, London, W.C.2
NORTH WESTERN PHILATELIC AUCTIONS LTD.,
    West Kirby, Wirral, Cheshire
PLUMRIDGE AND CO. LTD.,
    142 Strand, London, W.C.2
PUTTICK AND SIMPSON,
    7 Blenheim Street, New Bond Street, London, W.1
ROBSON LOWE LTD.,
    50 Pall Mall, London, S.W.1
WARREN SMITH,
    30 Maiden Lane, London, W.C.2
G. P. D. VESSEY LTD.,
    56A High Street, Whitstable, Kent
P. A. WILDE,
    21 Charles Street, Cardiff

INDEX

Provisionals, 50

Remainders, 40
Reprints, 41
Rouletting, 27

Siderography, 18
Stamps as currency, 52
Stereotyping, 16
Stock albums, 67
'Strips', 35, 64, 80

Telegraph stamps, 51
Thematic collections, 84–6
Tweezers, 65
Typography, 14

War-tax stamps, 52
Watermarks, 32–3
Watermark detectors, 68
Witherings, Thomas, 98–9
Writing-up, 75–6